Oxford School Shakespeare

The Merchant of Venice

edited by

Roma Gill
M.A. *Cantab*. B.Litt. *Oxon*.

DISCARDED

Oxford University Press

Oxford University Press, Walton Street, Oxford OX2 6DP

Oxford   New York
Athens   Auckland   Bangkok   Bombay
Calcutta   Cape Town   Dar es Salaam   Delhi
Florence   Hong Kong   Istanbul   Karachi
Kuala Lumpur   Madras   Madrid   Melbourne
Mexico City   Nairobi   Paris   Singapore
Taipei   Tokyo   Toronto

and associated companies in
Berlin   Ibadan

Oxford is a trade mark of Oxford University Press

© Oxford University Press 1979
First published 1979
Reprinted 1980, 1981, 1982, 1983, 1984, 1985, 1987 (twice), 1988,
1989, 1990, 1991, 1992
This revised edition first published 1992
Reprinted 1993, 1994, 1995

ISBN 0 19 831973 8

Illustrations by Coral Mula

Cover photograph by Richard H. Smith (Dominic Photography) shows
Dustin Hoffman as Shylock, Leigh Lawson as Antonio, and Geraldine
James as Portia, in Peter Hall Company's 1989 production of *The
Merchant of Venice*.

Oxford School Shakespeare
edited by Roma Gill

A Midsummer Night's Dream
Romeo and Juliet
As You Like It
Macbeth
Julius Caesar
The Merchant of Venice
Henry IV Part 1
Twelfth Night
The Taming of the Shrew
Othello
Hamlet
King Lear

Printed in Great Britain
at the University Press, Cambridge

Contents

Prejudice in *The Merchant of Venice* — v

Leading Characters in the Play — viii

The Merchant of Venice: commentary — x

Shylock — xxv

Shakespeare's Verse — xxix

Date and Text — xxx

Characters in the Play — xxxi

The Merchant of Venice — I

Sources — 91

Classwork and Examinations — 93
    Discussion — 93
    Character Study — 94
    Activities — 95
    Context Questions — 96
    Comprehension Questions — 98
    Essays — 100
    Projects — 101

Background — 102
    Government — 102
    Religion — 102
    Education — 103
    Language — 103
    Drama — 103
    Theatre — 104

Selected Further Reading — 105

William Shakespeare 1564–1616 — 106

List of Shakespeare's Plays — 108

Prejudice in *The Merchant of Venice*

Shylock, the money-lender who is hated because he is a Jew, explains how prejudice works. He calls it 'affection',[1] and shows the relationship between prejudice and the emotions:

> affection,
> Master of passion, sways it to the mood
> Of what it likes and loathes.

If we are prejudiced, we may dislike someone for no other reason than that he is different from us in nationality, religion, colour, or social class. In England today there are laws that attempt to control the effects of prejudice: it is an offence in law, for instance, for an employer to refuse a job simply because the applicant is coloured, or female, or Jewish. If *The Merchant of Venice* were a new play, written today, it would probably be censored by the Race Relations Board. The topics it presents—racial hatred, colour prejudice, class distinction, and the position of women in society—are all capable of provoking intense feelings in an audience; but this would not be the reason for the censor's disapproval. He would be suspicious of Shakespeare's attitude to these matters, as it is communicated through the characters and the action. Shakespeare seems to accept the prejudices of some of his characters. Only occasionally do they ever question the justice of their positions, and usually a satisfactory answer is to be found in subsequent events of the play.

Portia is one character who, at the beginning of the play, resents the situation in which she is placed. Her father, who is now dead, devised a test for selecting the man that his daughter should marry; in Portia's words, 'the will of a living daughter [is] curbed by the will of a dead father'. English girls today would find this intolerable, but Portia only grumbles: she does not rebel. Fortunately for Portia, the right man makes the right choice, and she is given to the man she loves. Portia does not think to question a man's right to the ownership of all his wife's possessions; in fact, she seems glad when she tells Bassanio,

[1] The word *affection* was quite often used in Shakespeare's time with this sense of 'prejudice'.

> But now I was the lord
> Of this fair mansion, master of my servants,
> Queen o'er myself; and even now, but now,
> This house, these servants, and this same myself
> Are yours, my lord's.

Only for the past hundred years has a woman in England been allowed to keep her own property when she marries, and even now there is some discrimination against the sex. Because I am a woman, I cannot borrow from a money-lender unless some man will act as guarantor for me, just as Antonio does for Bassanio.

The different social classes are clearly indicated in *The Merchant of Venice*, but the linguistic 'markers' that Shakespeare uses are not as familiar to a twentieth-century audience as they were to Shakespeare's contemporaries. The pronouns 'you' and 'thou' are very significant, and almost imperceptibly define the relationships between the characters. 'You' is neutral, formal, and polite, whilst 'thou' is affectionate, condescending, or contemptuous. Bassanio always speaks to Antonio as 'you', but to Gratiano as 'thou'; Antonio mostly uses the formal word, but with Bassanio he allows himself the occasional 'thou' of affection, and with Shylock the dismissive 'thou' of contempt. As long as Old Gobbo believes that he is speaking to a young gentleman, he adopts the 'you' which is appropriate when addressing a superior; but when he knows he is speaking to his son, his recognition is expressed through the pronoun: 'I'll be sworn if thou be Launcelot . . .'

It is by such small details that English social status is revealed. To show excessive care for position is ill-mannered, and the Prince of Arragon's lengthy discourse on rank shows him to be merely vulgar: he is himself the 'blinking idiot' that he finds in the casket.

Subtlety has no place, however, when colour is the object of the discrimination, and the Prince of Morocco wastes no words. He speaks proudly of his dark skin, the 'shadow'd livery of the burnish'd sun', and in his dignity we can feel Shakespeare's admiration for the character he has created and the people whom the Prince represents. Yet he is unacceptable as a suitor for Portia; her conversation with him leaves few doubts in our minds, and her relief when he chooses the wrong casket is unmistakeable: 'Let all of his complexion choose me so'.

The Prince of Morocco confronts Portia with a powerful argument against prejudice. Find a fair-skinned northern prince, he urges her, and let the two of them 'make incision' in their flesh. From both bodies, the blood that flows will be red. The argument is taken up in a later scene by Shylock, and the opening lines of Shylock's speech are often quoted to demonstrate Shakespeare's lack of prejudice and refusal to discriminate against individuals on grounds of race or religion.

> Hath not a Jew eyes? hath not a Jew hands, organs, dimensions, senses, affections, passions? Fed with the same food, hurt with the same weapons, subject to the same diseases, healed by the same means, warmed and cooled by the same winter and summer as a Christian is? If you prick us, do we not bleed?

But this can only serve as evidence when it is taken out of context— removed entirely from the play. *The Merchant of Venice* confirms Shylock as a villain, as monstrous a creature as any in the drama of Shakespeare's time. Indeed, English drama *since* the seventeenth century has failed to produce Shylock's equal.

The Jew was a figure hated and feared by the Elizabethans, but the reasons for their hatred are not at all simple. Superstition was a main one, arising out of medieval legends such as that of St. Hugh of Lincoln, a little boy who was said to have been crucified by Jews. True religious hostility was rare, but religion gave the English Christians a good excuse for persecuting the foreigners who had come to live amongst them. Dislike of the aliens was intensified by the prosperity of some Jews, whose success in business enterprises sometimes made the native English dependent on the immigrants. Parallel cases of suspicion and jealousy are not hard to find in the modern world.

Shylock's viciousness transcends his Jewishness, and it would be unfair to cite this character as an example of Shakespeare's racial prejudice. But we can find this surrounding Shylock's daughter. We are sympathetic to Jessica, yet we are never allowed to forget that she is a Jew. The reminders are always affectionate, and sometimes funny—as when Launcelot reproaches Lorenzo for converting Jessica, 'for in converting Jews to Christians you raise the price of pork'. Laughter can take away the cruelty of prejudice, but it helps to reinforce in an audience the awareness of difference.

In *The Merchant of Venice* Shakespeare acknowledges the existence of prejudice, and he makes use of it to suit his dramatic ends. He was an entertainer, not a reformer. His play cannot be read as propaganda for the abolition of prejudice; at most, it recommends that we should sometimes remember that there is a human being inside the skin.

Leading characters in the play

Antonio the merchant of the play's title. He is a good and generous man, who promises to pay Shylock the money borrowed by Bassanio or else allow Shylock to cut off a pound of his flesh. His part in the play is rather a passive one, and he reveals his character mainly in his generosity to his friend and in his hatred of the Jew.

Bassanio a younger man, who has already spent all his own money and now hopes to restore his fortunes by marrying an heiress. He needs to borrow money so that he can appear rich when he courts Portia, and it is for his sake that Antonio enters into the bond with Shylock. Bassanio is made to show good judgement when he makes his choice of the leaden casket and so wins Portia for his wife.

Gratiano a young man with a reputation for wild behaviour. He accompanies Bassanio to Belmont, and wins the love of Portia's lady-in-waiting, Nerissa.

Lorenzo He is in love with Jessica, and plans to steal her from her father's house.

Portia the most important character in the play. She is an heiress, and is in love with Bassanio; but her father has devised a test with three caskets, and Portia must marry the man who chooses the right casket. Portia is intelligent as well as beautiful; dressed as a lawyer she goes to Venice and saves Antonio from being killed by Shylock. Her home is Belmont, and the peace and harmony here contrast with the tense business world of Venice.

Nerissa Portia's lady-in-waiting, who falls in love with Gratiano. When Portia goes to Venice as a lawyer, Nerissa accompanies her, dressed as a lawyer's clerk.

Shylock a money-lender, who is hated for his greed and because he is a Jew. He is Antonio's enemy, and when Bassanio's money is not repaid he demands the pound of flesh that Antonio promised as a forfeit. (See also p. xxv.)

Jessica   Shylock's daughter; she disguises herself as a boy in order to run away from her father's house, where she is unhappy. She is in love with the Christian Lorenzo.

Launcelot Gobbo   the comedian of the play. He is at first Shylock's servant, then goes to work for Bassanio. His clowning often takes the form of misusing the English language; it is sometimes a welcome break from the tense or romantic scenes.

The Merchant of Venice: commentary

The action of the play takes place in Venice and in Belmont. Belmont is imaginary, but Venice is real. The city is located on the sea coast in the north of Italy, and is in fact built over a lagoon. Its main streets are canals, and the only vehicles are boats (see illustration page 13). In the sixteenth century, Venice was the centre for international trade, importing goods from all corners of the earth, and exporting them in the same way. We are told that Antonio, the greatest of the merchants, is waiting for his ships to return

> From Tripolis, from Mexico, and England,
> From Lisbon, Barbary, and India.   (3, 2, 267–8)

To be successful, a merchant had to invest his money wisely—and have luck on his side. Trading by sea was hazardous, and a sudden storm, or unseen rocks, could easily wreck a ship and drown the merchant's hopes along with the cargo.

Act 1

Scene 1   When his friends see that Antonio is depressed, they immediately think that he is worried about his ships at sea. They are sympathetic, and Solanio does his best to make light of the situation by exaggerating his fears to make his friend smile. But Antonio is sad for some other reason, and when we meet his dearest friend, Bassanio, we begin to guess at this reason. Bassanio is a carefree young man, who cheerfully admits that he has spent all of his own money and a good deal of Antonio's. However, Bassanio now has a scheme for acquiring more wealth. Before he gives any details, he explains his theory: a lost arrow (he says) can often be found by shooting another arrow in the same direction, and watching carefully to see where it falls. The theory is, as Bassanio acknowledges, a 'childhood proof'; he believed it when he was a schoolboy, and now he wants to put it to the test again, spending more money in the hope of winning back what he has lost. This is not a very sensible, or responsible, way to act, but Bassanio emphasizes his youth and innocence. Perhaps he hopes that Antonio will treat him as though he were a child, and ignore the irresponsibility of his demand for more money to spend.

Bassanio next tells Antonio of an heiress, who has already given him some unspoken encouragement. Her name is Portia, and Bassanio claims to have fallen in love with her. He may be speaking the truth, but it is clear that the lady's wealth is a very attractive feature for him. Antonio promises aid, but all the money he possesses is tied up in his own business ventures. Still, his 'credit' is good, and Bassanio can borrow all the ducats he needs to present himself to Portia as an eligible suitor, giving Antonio's name as security—that is, promising that Antonio will repay the debt if he himself is unable to do so.

Our feelings towards Bassanio at the end of this scene cannot be wholly favourable, despite his youthful optimism. He has wasted a lot of money, both his own and his friend's. It seems that he wants to marry Portia not just because of love but also because of her money. But he himself, perhaps unconsciously, shows what we should feel about him when he explains that his youth has been 'something too prodigal'. Repeated phrases throughout the play compare Bassanio with the Prodigal Son of Christ's parable (St. Luke 15: 11-32), who spent all his inheritance in 'riotous living'. When he was penniless and starving, he went repentantly back to his father's house, where he was welcomed with rejoicing. Bassanio has been 'prodigal'; now he asks for a chance to redeem himself.

Like the Prodigal Son's father, Antonio has shown the loving and forgiving generosity of his nature, but he remains a mysterious character. Early in the scene he tells Gratiano that he thinks of the world as 'A stage where every man must play a part, And mine a sad one'. It is his changing relationship with Bassanio that causes his melancholy. Some Elizabethans thought—as the Greeks and Romans did—that the friendship between two men was a more spiritual bond, and should be more highly esteemed, than the love between a man and a woman. Knowing that Bassanio is interested in a lady (see lines 119-21), Antonio may be secretly grieving for the inevitable end to a friendship.

Scene 2　　　　　From the hearty, but anxious, masculine world of Venice, we move to the feminine peace of Belmont. Even here there is anxiety, as Portia's opening sigh indicates. It is now Nerissa who tries to cheer Portia, but she cannot take her mistress's mind off the situation where she is surrounded by suitors and yet 'cannot choose one, nor refuse none'. Shakespeare has to communicate to his audience a lot of information about the trial that Portia's father devised for the men who wish to marry her. The information is given gradually, in five separate scenes, so that we seem to discover the facts just as the suitors do. For the moment, we are merely told that each candidate must make a choice between three caskets.

Nerissa explains why Portia must obey this somewhat absurd commandment when she says that 'holy men at their death have good inspirations'. It was proverbially believed that a good man would be divinely inspired, and might even speak prophetically, when he was close to death. To disobey or disregard such an utterance was almost sacrilege.

The two young women amuse themselves by gossiping about the suitors who have already assembled at Belmont. Although Portia and Nerissa are Italian, they share a sense of humour which is undoubtedly English. As they laugh about each man's peculiarities, we can learn something of what the Elizabethan Englishmen thought of their continental neighbours—and also of how they could laugh at themselves. The 'young baron of England' is a caricature of the Englishman abroad, in the twentieth century as well as in the sixteenth: the English have never been good at speaking foreign languages! Nor is there a 'national dress' for England, such as many other countries possess; the Englishman was always content (it seems) to imitate the costumes of other countries. The joke about the Scottish lord would have a topical significance for Shakespeare's audience. At this time England and Scotland were separate kingdoms, and in their frequent quarrels the French always promised to aid the Scots (but rarely kept their promises).

We are never allowed to see this 'parcel of wooers', for Nerissa tells Portia that they have all decided to return home, not trying their luck with the caskets. There is no doubt that Portia is glad they are leaving. Nerissa reminds her of a young Venetian whom Portia met whilst her father was alive, and the promptness with which Portia recalls Bassanio's name is enough to tell us that she remembers him with pleasure. Bassanio is described by Nerissa as 'a scholar and a soldier'. These qualities made up the ideal courtier in Elizabethan eyes, and the description may help to prepare us for a Bassanio who is rather different from the one we left in Venice.

Portia's enthusiasm dies away, and her weary resignation returns, when she is told that a new suitor is approaching Belmont. It is the Prince of Morocco, and the title arouses her prejudice as she goes inside to prepare for his coming.

Scene 3   Meanwhile, in Venice, Bassanio has found a usurer who can lend the money he needs. Shylock is very cautious, repeating each of Bassanio's demands to make sure that they are perfectly understood. His deliberation makes Bassanio nervous, and he shows irritation when Shylock says that 'Antonio is a good man'. The word 'good' has different implications: Bassanio thinks that it refers to Antonio's character, and he is angry that such a man as Shylock should presume to judge his friend. Shylock, having succeeded in annoying Bassanio, hastens to explain that by 'good' he meant only 'sufficient'—financially sound. The two disagree again over the interpretation of 'assur'd', by which Bassanio means that Shylock may trust Antonio; Shylock says that he will indeed be 'assur'd', meaning that he will take all precautions to protect himself and his money.

Bassanio's polite invitation to dinner is refused by Shylock in words that introduce the theme of racial hatred: he thinks he would be asked 'to smell pork', a meat forbidden to Jews by their religion. Shylock perhaps speaks these words '*aside*', not talking directly to Bassanio but uttering his thoughts aloud for the audience alone to hear them, just as only the audience hears the soliloquy in which Shylock reveals his attitude to Antonio. Religious feeling has some part in this attitude, but a minor one compared with the enmity he bears towards a business rival.

We learn that Antonio disapproves morally of lending money for interest (and it is a mark of his affection for Bassanio that he is prepared now to break his own rules). Shylock justifies his activities by telling the story of Jacob from the Old Testament (Genesis 30: 31–43). Jacob was angry with Laban, his uncle, and tried to outwit him, using his skill as a shepherd. He believed that the ewes, seeing the striped twigs in front of them when they conceived, would give birth to striped or spotted lambs, which Laban had agreed should become Jacob's wages. This indeed happened, but whereas Shylock applauds Jacob's cunning, Antonio (and most devout Jews) ascribes the success to the hand of God.

The merchant and the usurer engage in passionate argument. Shylock reveals the cruel insults he has had to suffer from Antonio in the past, but Antonio stands firm in his contempt for the Jew.

He refuses to borrow the money as a friend, but urges Shylock, with words that he will regret, to

> lend it rather to thine enemy;
> Who if he break, thou may'st with better face
> Exact the penalty.

Shylock proposes 'a merry sport' which Antonio, surprisingly, is willing to accept. He agrees to the forfeit that Shylock suggests—'an equal pound of your fair flesh'—to be given if the money cannot be properly repaid.

The words 'kind' and 'kindness' are repeated several times at the end of this scene. They have a surface meaning—'generous' and 'generosity'—which Antonio accepts, and an ironic double meaning. If Shylock 'grows kind' in this second sense, he will become even more like himself, true to his nature. And we have already, in his soliloquy, seen what this is.

Act 2

Scene 1   Prejudice is the subject of the short episode in Belmont, where we see Portia's reception of the Prince of Morocco. The prince's appearance shows that he is an exotic figure: a note, probably written by Shakespeare himself, describes him as 'a tawny [brown] Moor, all in white'. His first speech reinforces our sense that he is excitingly different from the Europeans that we have seen so far, but it does not change Portia's mind. She is polite, but we understand, better than Morocco can, what she means when she tells him that, in her eyes, he is 'as fair As any comer I have look'd on yet'. We have heard what Portia thought of her other suitors. The Prince's reply to this ambiguous remark does not encourage our good opinion of him. He boasts of his own valour and achievements in very exaggerated language, and so loses some of our sympathy.

We are given a new piece of information concerning the casket test. The men who choose wrongly must never again think of marrying. It is now clear why the earlier suitors left Belmont without trying their luck; Morocco, however, is not deterred, and prepares to make his choice.

Whilst Morocco is taking his oath in the 'temple'—many great houses at this time had their own private chapels—Shakespeare returns us to Venice. The next five scenes will send Bassanio from Venice to Belmont, and introduce a sub-plot, connected to the main plot through Jessica, Shylock's daughter. First, Shakespeare creates a role for the leading comedian of his acting company: he is to be Launcelot Gobbo, Shylock's servant.

Scene 2   Comedy scenes such as this are the most difficult and un-rewarding to read; they need to be performed, so that the actor can introduce the visual effects that the lines demand. When Launcelot pretends to be torn between his conscience and the devil, he might (for instance) jump to the left when the devil is speaking—because devils traditionally appeared on the left—and to the right when 'conscience' replies. There could be humour in the difference between Launcelot's appearance (as the miserly Shylock's servant he would not be well dressed) and his grand manner of speech to the old man; this would emphasize the comedy of the 'mistaken identity' situation. When Old Gobbo feels his son's head and comments on his 'beard', it is obvious from Launce-lot's reply that he has got hold of the hair tied at the back of his neck; and if Launcelot passes his father's hand across his fingers, implying that they are his ribs ('You may tell every finger I have with my ribs'), the comedy will increase with the old man's bewilderment.

The English language is a very complicated one, and English-men themselves are not always very good at speaking it! There are many words that sound grand—but sometimes the people who use them do not understand their meanings, or else confuse one word with another that sounds similar. This is especially likely to happen when the speakers are trying to create a good impression of themselves. Launcelot and his father are doing this when they address Bassanio. They are conscious that Bassanio is a gentleman, whilst they are only peasants, and they try to use what they think is the proper language of gentlemen. Even in the twentieth century, when class distinctions are much less clearly marked than they were in the sixteenth, the writers of television comedy still find subjects for laughter in our linguistic snobbishness. Lorenzo's comment is valid today: 'How every fool can play upon the word' (*3, 5, 42*).

Bassanio is in a good temper, and responds well to Launcelot's fooling; he agrees to employ him and give him 'a livery More guarded than his fellows'. A 'guarded' uniform—one decorated with yellow braid—was often worn by the professional fool in a gentleman's household; perhaps this is the function that Bassanio intends for Launcelot when he becomes 'The follower of so poor a gentleman'.

Even though he admits he is poor, Bassanio is already behaving with his former extravagance, now that he has got Shylock's money. He is planning to give a party before he leaves Venice. However, he shows a more sedate side of his character when Gratiano asks to accompany him to Belmont. Gratiano turns Bassanio's solemn warning into comedy. He promises to behave in a way that is very sober, but at the same time quite ridiculous, and he probably accompanies his speech with exaggerated gestures.

Scene 3   Quickly, Shakespeare presents his new plot when Jessica gives to Launcelot the letter she has written to Lorenzo. The short scene takes the plot one small step further, and it also serves to increase our dislike for Shylock. We learn that his 'house is hell', and that Jessica is 'asham'd to be [her] father's child', although she recognizes that it is a 'heinous sin' for a daughter to have such feelings.

Scene 4   The letter is delivered to Lorenzo when he and his friends are discussing their costumes for Bassanio's party. It was quite usual, in Shakespeare's time, for a small band of the guests at a grand feast to disguise themselves in elaborate costumes and entertain the other guests with a masque—a performance with singing and dancing. Page-boys carried torches for the masquers, and Lorenzo suddenly realizes how he can steal Jessica away from her father's house: she can be disguised as his page.

Scene 5   There can scarcely be a greater contrast than that between the lively young men planning their evening's entertainment, and the surly Shylock. He takes no pleasure in the feast, but has decided to 'go in hate, to feed upon The prodigal Christian' (yet another comparison of Bassanio with the Prodigal Son). Shylock is determined to do all he can to ruin Bassanio, and he even considers that Launcelot's change of employer might 'help to waste His borrow'd purse'.

Scene 6   Gratiano's reference to the 'penthouse' under which they are standing is one of many remarks in Elizabethan drama that help us to reconstruct, in imagination, the kind of stage that Shakespeare was writing for. It seems that there was always a balcony, which allowed 'split-level' acting. In this scene the young men assemble on the main stage, underneath the 'penthouse' formed by the balcony on which Jessica appears, dressed as a boy. She is shy, because in Elizabethan times women *never* wore men's clothes. Her embarrassment is expressed with great delicacy, and it is easy to forget that Shakespeare and his contemporaries would probably have been a little amused by the situation. In many plays of this period the female characters put on masculine clothing, and a gentle comedy arises out of the fact that female characters were always played by boy actors: the boys dress up as girls, and then the 'girls' turn into boys.

Waiting for Jessica has made the masquers late for the feast, and now Antonio comes in search of Gratiano. The wind has changed, and it is time to set sail for Belmont.

Scene 7   Whilst all the activity of Jessica's elopement was taking place in Venice, the Prince of Morocco at Belmont has dined, and sworn an oath never to look for a wife if he fails the casket test. At last we see the caskets that we have heard so much about. Each one bears an inscription, which Morocco reads aloud. The gold and silver caskets make promises, but the leaden one is menacing. Morocco refuses to be threatened, and passes to the silver casket, which assures him that he 'shall get as much as he deserves'. We heard in *Act 2*, scene 1 that he has a good opinion of himself, and he is naturally tempted to choose silver. The golden casket, however, offers 'what many men desire', and Morocco decides that this refers to Portia, because 'all the world desires her'. It would be an insult to Portia (he concludes) to associate her with lead, or even with silver; so he opens the golden casket.

The casket contains a skull, the emblem of death—which indeed many unhappy men do desire. Shocked and saddened, the Prince of Morocco departs immediately.

Scene 8   In Venice, Shylock has discovered that his daughter is missing—and she has taken a lot of his money with her. Solanio gives a comical account of the Jew's confusion, when Shylock apparently did not know which loss to lament more. It is important that we do not *see* Shylock here, because his distress might create too much sympathy for him. Instead, we join Salerio and Solanio in their laughter.

But not everything in this scene is comic: there is bad news for Antonio. A ship has been wrecked in the English Channel, and it may well be his. The conversation becomes sober, as the two friends think of Antonio's generosity—'A kinder gentleman treads not the earth'—and remind us of his great affection for Bassanio: 'I think he only loves the world for him'.

Scene 9   Yet another suitor, the Prince of Arragon, has arrived at Belmont; he repeats the three promises that he has sworn to keep, and goes to make his choice of the three caskets. Like the Prince of Morocco, he reads the inscriptions, and speaks his thoughts aloud.

The Prince of Arragon is excessively conscious of his social position, and insists that he is different from other men: he will not 'jump with common spirits', and look in the golden casket for 'what many men desire'. He is attracted by the promise of the silver casket: 'Who chooseth me shall get as much as he deserves'. For a time he meditates on the subject of nobility and merit, deploring the fact that 'low peasantry' (men of humble birth) can be found among noblemen—'the true seed of honour'. Having convinced *himself* that he deserves to win Portia, he opens the silver casket. We are not surprised that this is the wrong choice, for Arragon has convinced *us* that he is far too conceited—although perhaps he deserves something better than 'the portrait of a blinking idiot'.

As soon as the Prince of Arragon has left, news is brought that another suitor is approaching. He has already made a good impression on Portia's servants with the 'Gifts of rich value' that he has sent to announce his coming; and we recognize the extravagance that is characteristic of Bassanio. Portia and Nerissa are hopeful.

Act 3

Scene 1   The optimism of Belmont gives place to the darkening atmosphere of Venice. There is still no confirmation that the ship wrecked in the English Channel is indeed Antonio's, but Solanio believes the rumour to be true. Shylock also has heard the report, and his anger over his daughter's flight is forgotten for a moment as he gives expression to his hatred and resentment of Antonio. He has had to suppress his feelings for years, but now they explode violently. His passion increases, and so too does the sympathy of the audience. He appeals to common humanity: 'Hath not a Jew eyes? hath not a Jew hands . . . if you poison us, do we not die?' He becomes almost a hero, and certainly a human being—then suddenly he changes back into a monster: 'and if you wrong us, shall we not revenge?'

Salerio and Solanio are fortunately saved from having to reply to this tirade; they leave Shylock with another Jew, Tubal, who has news of Jessica.

Shylock experiences another confusion of emotions as Tubal imparts various pieces of information in an incoherent manner. Jessica is spending her father's money recklessly, and in exchange for a pet monkey she has given away the ring that was a token of betrothal from her mother to her father. Grief and anger conflict with malicious glee when Shylock hears of Antonio's misfortunes, and it is clear that he will take revenge for the loss of his daughter and his ring when he claims the forfeit from Antonio.

Scene 2 Portia is happy in Bassanio's company, and she tries to persuade him to stay at Belmont for a few days before making his choice of the caskets. Her happiness is mingled with modesty, for she is too shy to tell Bassanio that she loves him. Bassanio too has fallen in love, but he cannot endure the uncertainty and feels that he must try his luck as soon as possible. So Portia orders Nerissa and the servants to stand aside, away from the caskets. Portia and Bassanio seem to be alone on the stage. Music is playing, whilst Portia watches the man she loves as he tries to make the decision that will bring happiness to both of them.

The song that helps to create a magic atmosphere also introduces Bassanio's meditation on appearance and reality. He is speaking only to himself; Portia does not hear him, just as he did not hear her speech before the song. The audience, of course, knows which casket Bassanio must choose, because Shakespeare has already shown us the contents of the gold and silver caskets.

Portia is almost overcome with delight when Bassanio selects the 'meagre lead'; and when Bassanio finds 'Fair Portia's counterfeit' in the casket he is ecstatically happy. He praises the picture rapturously, and for a time cannot believe his luck.

A rather more materialistic note is heard in the metaphorical language when Portia wishes to 'stand high in [Bassanio's] *account*', and offers him 'the full *sum*' of herself; it is repeated when Gratiano refers to the '*bargain*' of their faith. But to balance this there is the ritual moment when Portia gives away all that she owns (including 'this same myself') and as a token places a ring on Bassanio's finger. Bassanio accepts the token, and binds himself to Portia:

when this ring
Parts from this finger, then parts life from hence.

Gratiano and Nerissa announce their intention of imitating Bassanio and Portia; and the happiness of the moment is complete.

It is now time to change the direction of the scene, and Shakespeare switches the mood with a bawdy joke (in prose).

The arrival of Salerio, Lorenzo, and Jessica is a welcome surprise, but the letter that Salerio has brought from Venice 'steals the colour from Bassanio's cheek'. Things have gone very badly for Antonio: he is ruined. Salerio can tell of Shylock's eagerness to claim his bond from Antonio, and Jessica is able to bear witness of her father's fiendish malice: 'he would rather have Antonio's flesh Than twenty times the value of the sum That he did owe him'. Portia is more than able to pay back the three thousand ducats, but we can take no comfort from her offer. The situation seems hopeless, and when Antonio's pathetic letter is read aloud it destroys the last remaining scrap of the happiness established in the scene.

Scene 3   A short scene shows us what the letter described. Antonio, in the custody of a gaoler, meets Shylock. The Jew will hear no pleas for mercy, and Antonio knows that it is useless to speak to him. Solanio hopes that the Duke will be able to intervene in the dispute, but Antonio knows the importance of strict justice in the mercantile world of which Venice is the head. This is a subject that will be mentioned at Antonio's trial.

Scene 4   Lorenzo has been telling Portia about Antonio, and Portia has decided that she and Nerissa will go away for a few days, leaving Belmont in the care of Lorenzo. She sends a servant to her cousin in Padua, asking for some 'notes and garments'. We understand the request for clothes when Portia explains to Nerissa that they are going to dress up as men, and that she herself will imitate all the mannerisms of a brash young man—including the voice that is 'between the change of man and boy'.

Scene 5   The next scene, still at Belmont, does nothing to develop any plot. But it encourages the audience to imagine that enough time has passed to allow Portia and Nerissa to travel from Belmont to Venice; on a practical level, it gives the actors time to change from their female dresses to the male costumes required in the following scene. In addition, it provides an opportunity for the comedian, in the part of Launcelot, to deliver some more of his word-play jokes. Launcelot, of course, accompanied his new master when Bassanio came to Belmont.

Act 4

Scene 1   The trial scene in *The Merchant of Venice* is the most famous scene in English drama. It has given a phrase to the English language: people who have never read the play—and perhaps never even heard of it—understand what it means to want one's 'pound of flesh'.

The conversation between the Duke and Antonio, before Shylock comes on to the stage, shows the hopeless resignation with which Antonio faces Shylock's wrath. The Duke makes a further plea for mercy, but Shylock is unmoved. He will admit that his hatred for Antonio is irrational and emotional: just as some people hate cats, or the sound of bagpipes, so (he says)

> can I give no reason, nor I will not,
> More than a lodg'd hate and a certain loathing
> I bear Antonio.

Antonio is not intimidated, and shows his contempt for Shylock's 'Jewish heart'. Bassanio offers to repay twice the money that he borrowed, but Shylock will not yield, and reminds the court that the pound of flesh is his by law. If the Duke refuses to grant this, it will appear that 'There is no force in the decrees of Venice'. We remember Antonio's words (*3*, 3, 27-31), and realize that, if the law is not observed, Venice will suffer in its reputation as the centre of international trade.

The Duke has made a final attempt to save Antonio legally. He has asked for the opinion of a famous lawyer, Bellario, and the court waits to hear this man's judgement. Bassanio is optimistic, but the tension of the situation has made Antonio even more resigned to his fate; he almost feels that he deserves to die.

The lawyer's clerk has brought a letter from Bellario, and whilst the Duke reads the letter, Shylock sharpens his knife. Gratiano cannot bear to see this sight, and he begins to abuse Shylock. The Jew appears to be unaffected by his insults, for he knows the strength of his position: 'I stand here for law'.

Bellario is sick, and cannot come to Venice; instead he has sent a legal colleague, 'a young doctor of Rome', who is fully acquainted with the case. The audience recognizes this 'doctor': it is Portia, and the 'clerk' was Nerissa. The other characters of the play, however, cannot penetrate the disguise.

Portia upholds Venetian law, but she urges Shylock to show

mercy. She describes the 'quality of mercy' as a divine blessing, which benefits both the man who shows mercy and the man who receives it. The petition in the Lord's Prayer, 'forgive us our trespasses', comes to mind when Portia explains how mercy belongs to God; if this were not so, the whole human race would be damned for its sins. But this is Christian doctrine, and Shylock's religion is of the Old Testament, which emphasizes the importance of the law, just as Shylock does now: 'I crave the law'.

Once again Bassanio offers the money; again Shylock refuses it; and once more we are reminded that a general principle lies beneath this particular instance:

> 'Twill be recorded for a precedent,
> And many an error by the same example
> Will rush into the state.

The statement is harsh, but it is correct. Portia has earned Shylock's praise 'A Daniel come to judgement'. Daniel was 'a young youth', according to 'The Story of Susanna' in the *Apocrypha*. He was inspired by God to give judgement when the chaste Susanna was accused of adultery by two lascivious 'elders' who had tried to rape her.

Portia continues to win Shylock's approval as she instructs the court about the penalty that Antonio must pay. The knife is sharpened, and the scales are ready; Antonio prepares for death. He speaks a few words of comfort to Bassanio, ending with a wry jest about the debt:

> For if the Jew do cut but deep enough,
> I'll pay it instantly with all my heart.

The tension is broken, but only for a moment, when Bassanio and Gratiano refer to their wives. The 'lawyer' and his 'clerk' are amused.

Just when Shylock is ready to cut into Antonio's flesh, Portia stops the proceedings. She reveals to Shylock the single flaw in his carefully worded bond: he is entitled to his pound of flesh, but has made no provision for a single drop of blood.

Gratiano exults over Shylock, repeating ironically all the words of praise that the Jew bestowed on the 'learned judge', and agreeing that he is indeed 'A second Daniel'. Like Portia, Daniel was not expected in the court, and the verdict he gave saved Susanna and condemned her accusers. The comparison is more apt now than it was when Shylock introduced it.

Shylock realizes that he cannot have his pound of flesh, and he tries to take the money that Bassanio is still offering. Now it is Portia's turn to be inflexible, and she insists that Shylock can have 'merely justice, and his bond'. When Shylock proposes to leave the court, Portia calls him back. The law of Venice has a strict penalty that must be paid by any 'alien'—foreigner—who tries to murder a Venetian. Shylock has thus offended, and for this crime his possessions are confiscated and his life is in danger. Antonio, of course, shows his generosity. Half of Shylock's wealth is forfeited to him, but he is willing to renounce his personal share and take the money on loan, keeping it in trust for Lorenzo, 'the gentleman That lately stole his daughter'. He makes two conditions: firstly, Shylock must become a Christian; and, secondly, he must make a will leaving all that he possesses to Jessica and Lorenzo. Shylock is utterly defeated. He asks for permission to leave the court, and indicates his agreement to Antonio's conditions: 'send the deed after me And I will sign it'.

For a long time Bassanio has been silent, perhaps because the events have affected him very deeply and prevented him from sharing in Gratiano's expressions of triumph. Sometimes Gratiano's speeches seem rather cruel, for although Shylock undoubtedly deserves punishment, it is hard that he should lose everything, including his right to believe in the Jewish faith. Gratiano, however, shows the character that Bassanio rebuked him for before the two men went to Belmont—'bold of voice' and with a 'skipping spirit' (2, 2, 173; 179). Bassanio and Antonio are more dignified in their behaviour.

It is only necessary now to pay the 'lawyer', and then Bassanio can take Antonio home to Belmont, to meet his new wife. The 'lawyer' refuses payment, then suddenly catches sight of a ring on Bassanio's finger, and requests this as a keepsake. It is the ring that Portia gave to Bassanio, telling him that if he should ever part with it for any reason, it would 'presage the ruin of [his] love'. Remembering this, Bassanio refuses; the 'lawyer' departs, apparently angry. Antonio begs Bassanio not to withhold the ring, and Bassanio cannot refuse the friend who risked so much for him.

Scene 2   Gratiano hurries after Portia to give her Bassanio's ring. Nerissa, still disguised as the lawyer's clerk, whispers to Portia that she will use a similar trick to get her own ring from Gratiano. The two girls laugh in anticipation of their husbands' embarrassment when they return to Belmont.

Act 5

Scene 1   Moonlight and music emphasize the tranquillity of Belmont and its contrast with the harsh legal world of Venice. Lorenzo and Jessica are relaxed here, and Jessica's escape from the 'hell' of her father's house seems to be almost as remote in time as the mythological lovers who are recalled by the moonlight. The mood of the scene is saved from being over-romantic when the couple start to tease each other, and when the messengers break in with their news. Harmony is restored, however, when Lorenzo and Jessica are alone again. Lorenzo starts to explain the theory of the music of the spheres, which Plato (a Greek philosopher) described. The music was made as the spheres touched each other in their constant motion, but could not be heard by human ears, which are deafened by the noises of earthly life.

Portia's musicians appear, probably on the balcony, to 'draw [their mistress] home with music'. The beauty of Lorenzo's speech (when he describes the 'patens of bright gold', and the 'young-eyed cherubins') blends with the playing of the musicians to re-create, in human terms, the heavenly harmony. Lorenzo and Jessica fall silent; perhaps they are asleep.

Portia and Nerissa come from the opposite side of the stage as they approach Belmont from Venice. Their chatter breaks into the music, and the dream world becomes real. A trumpet announces the arrival of Bassanio, just as day is breaking. The missing rings provide a final gentle comedy, as the two embarrassed husbands try to justify their actions to wives who are trying to hide their amusement.

In the end, of course, all is happiness. Lorenzo and Jessica join the other two couples, and Portia gives Antonio a last surprise —the news that three of his ships 'Are richly come to harbour suddenly'. There can be no reaction from the audience other than Antonio's 'I am dumb', and final applause for Shakespeare. He has taken three main strands—the casket story, the bond story, and the ring story—and woven them into a single plot, which brings all three stories to a successful conclusion, and ensures that all the characters—with one exception—'live happily ever after', just as fairy-tale characters ought to do.

Shylock

A happy ending for the leading characters is essential for a romantic comedy such as *The Merchant of Venice*. But one very important character is left out of the general rejoicing in Act 5. Shylock has been defeated of his bond, robbed of his ducats, and deserted by his daughter; he is even compelled to give up his birthright, his Jewish religion, and become one of the Christians whom he so much hates. Does he deserve this fate? Is *The Merchant of Venice* a comedy for all the other characters, but a tragedy for Shylock?

Shakespeare took the story of Shylock's bond from an Italian novel, but the money-lending Jew in this source has no personality, and no daughter. Consequently, we can assume that Shylock is Shakespeare's own creation: all the personality traits that we find in him were deliberately worked out by the dramatist, and not borrowed accidentally along with the plot.

Shylock starts from a double disadvantage, as far as an Elizabethan audience was concerned. He is a Jew, and he is a money-lender. There were not many Jews in England, but in the Middle Ages English Christians hated the Jews, and this feeling was still strong in the sixteenth century. The Elizabethans also hated the traditional Jewish profession of usury—the lending of money for profit. Jews were often forbidden to own land or to engage in trade in England; consequently the only lucrative profession open to them was money-lending. The Christians deplored this—in theory. In practice, the expanding economy of the times demanded that money should be readily available. Francis Bacon, who was Lord Chancellor of England in 1618, claimed that

> to speak of the abolishing of usury is idle. All states have ever had it, in one kind, or rate, or other. So as that opinion must be sent to Utopia.　　　　　　　　　　(Essay 'Of Usury')

Certainly, the usurer is necessary to the world of *The Merchant of Venice*. Shylock's wealth is evidence of his professional success, which could only come from satisfying a social need.

Shylock first appears as the cautious businessman, thinking carefully before he invests his three thousand ducats in Bassanio's

enterprise. His reaction to the polite invitation to dinner is un-
expected in its venom, which increases as he tells the audience of
his hatred for Antonio. Religious differences seem to be less
important than professional jealousy:

> I hate him for he is a Christian;
> But more for that in low simplicity
> He lends out money gratis.

To some extent Shylock justifies his hostility when he describes
how he has been treated by Antonio—insulted, spat upon, and
kicked out of the way like 'a stranger cur'. Because of this, we
sympathize with him. When the scene ends, we are left with two
conflicting opinions of Shylock and his 'merry sport'. Are we to
share Antonio's surprise, 'And say there is much kindness in the
Jew'? Or is Bassanio right to be suspicious of 'fair terms and a
villain's mind'?

The scene with Antonio and Bassanio shows Shylock in his
professional, public, life. Next, we hear what he is like at home.
His comic servant, Launcelot Gobbo, exaggerates (with a characteristic misuse of the English language) when he says that 'the Jew
is the very devil incarnation'. But this opinion is echoed by Shylock's daughter, Jessica, when she sighs 'Our house is hell'. Jessica
is 'asham'd to be [her] father's child', although she knows that it
is a 'heinous sin' for a daughter to have such feelings. We can
understand Jessica's misery when her father gives instructions
about locking up his house whilst he is away. Jessica is forbidden
even to look out of the window to watch the masquers going to
Bassanio's feast. Shylock is a kill-joy—and he has also killed his
daughter's natural affection for him.

Shakespeare does not let us see Shylock in his first frenzy of
distress when he finds that Jessica is missing, because this would
surely arouse our sympathy. Instead, Solanio describes the scene,
and the audience is encouraged to share in his laughter. From
Solanio's account, it seems that Shylock's grief over the loss of his
daughter is equalled (perhaps even surpassed) by his anger at the
theft of his money. He utters 'a passion so confus'd':

> My daughter! O my ducats! O my daughter!
> Fled with a Christian! O my Christian ducats!

When Shylock next appears (*Act 3*, scene 1) the passion is subdued
into an intense and malevolent bitterness; yet the jesting of the

two Christians is cruel. The loss of a daughter is a real cause for sorrow, and Shylock earns some pity (from the audience) when he tells Solanio and Salerio that 'my daughter is my flesh and my blood'.

It is with very mixed feelings, then, that we are led up to the powerful speech in which Shylock catalogues the abuses he has had to suffer from Christians in general, and from Antonio in particular. There is only one reason that he can see for this treatment: 'I am a Jew'. It is easy to respond to the rhetorical questions that follow:

> Hath not a Jew eyes? hath not a Jew hands, organs, dimensions, senses, affections, passions? fed with the same food, hurt with the same weapons, subject to the same diseases, healed by the same means, warmed and cooled by the same winter and summer, as a Christian is? if you prick us, do we not bleed? if you tickle us, do we not laugh? if you poison us, do we not die?

Shylock appeals to our common humanity. To give a negative answer to his questions would deny not *his* humanity, but our own. The speech, however, continues:

> and if you wrong us, shall we not revenge? If we are like you in the rest, we will resemble you in that . . . The villainy you teach me I will execute, and it shall go hard but I will better the instruction.

Common humanity ignores all limitations of colour, race, or creed; and this is strongly asserted in the first part of Shylock's speech. But the assertions of these last lines show that the individual—Shylock—is determined to ignore the limits of humanity. He will 'better the instruction', and prove himself to be not the *equal* of the Christians in inflicting suffering on others, but their *superior*.

The events that follow do nothing to moderate the presentation of Shylock in the terms used by the Duke when he warns Antonio, before the trial begins, that his adversary is

> an inhuman wretch
> Uncapable of pity, void and empty
> From any dram of mercy.

During the trial, Shylock loses the audience's sympathy, by his words and by the action of sharpening the knife on the sole of his shoe (which Gratiano observes in line 123). Neither insults nor pleading spoil the enjoyment of his triumph, and when sentence is given against Antonio, he repeats the words of the bond with a lingering relish:

> Ay, 'his breast':
> So says the bond—doth it not, noble judge?—
> 'Nearest his heart'—those are the very words.

Shylock demanded a strict observance of the law, and (in poetic justice) it is precisely this that defeats him. Gratiano exults over his downfall, but the other characters in the court speak no unnecessary words and show no satisfaction until Shylock has left the court. Even then, conversation is formal, occupied only with thanks and payment. It does not obliterate the memory of Shylock's parting words:

> I pray you give me leave to go from hence:
> I am not well.

A snarl of frustrated wrath can deliver this line; or else it can be spoken with the anguish of a man who has lost everything—his daughter, his wealth, his religious freedom, and the engagement ring given to him by his wife.

Recent English productions of *The Merchant of Venice* have emphasized the suffering human being, but I do not think that this is what Shakespeare intended. Shylock is more complex than any of the other characters in the play: we can think of him as a 'real' person, whose words and deeds are motivated by thoughts and feelings that we can discover from the play, and that we can understand when we have discovered them. We cannot think of Bassanio (for instance) in this way. Yet in admiring Shakespeare's achievement in the creation of Shylock, we must beware of danger. Often, when we know a person well, and understand why he acts as he does, we become sympathetic to him; in *The Merchant of Venice* we are further encouraged to sympathize with Shylock also by the fact that other leading characters (such as Bassanio) do *not* compel our sympathies. Sympathy can give rise to affection, and affection often tempts us to withhold moral judgement, or at least be gentle in our censure. Shylock's conduct merits condemnation. We can only refrain from condemning it because we know that he has suffered for being a Jew; and this, surely, is another form of prejudice?

Shakespeare's Verse

Shakespeare's plays are mainly written in 'blank verse', the form preferred by most dramatists in the sixteenth and early seventeenth centuries. It is a very flexible medium, which is capable — like the human speaking voice — of a wide range of tones. Basically, the lines, which are unrhymed, are ten syllables long. The syllables have alternating stresses, just like normal English speech; and they divide into five 'feet'. The technical name for this is 'iambic pentameter'.

Solanio

Beliéve me, sír, had Í such vénture fórth,
The bétter párt of mý afféctions woúld
Be with my hópes abroad. I shoúld be stíll
Plúcking the gráss to knów where síts the wínd;
Péering in máps for pórts, and piérs, and róads;
And évery óbject thát might máke me feár
Misfórtune tó my véntures, oút of doúbt
Would máke me sád.

Salerio

My wínd, coolíng my bróth,
Would blów me tó an águe, whén I thought
What hárm a wínd too gréat might dó at seá.

1, 1, 15–24

Here the pentameter accommodates a variety of speech tones — Solanio starts with the simple, conversational expression 'Believe me'; then his speech becomes more dramatic as his imagination takes hold of the subject. Salerio, speaking on the same theme, joins in halfway through a line, as though he were singing the same tune as Solanio.

In this quotation, the lines are fairly regular in length and mostly normal in iambic stress pattern. Solanio's 'every' must be given only two syllables ('ev'ry') as in much modern English speech; and the stresses on 'Plucking' and 'Peering' are not iambic — and the irregularity seems to emphasize his own little drama.

Sometimes the verse line contains the grammatical unit of meaning — 'Peering in maps for ports, and piers, and roads' —

thus allowing for a pause at the end of the line, before a new idea is started; at other times, the sense runs on from one line to the next — 'I should be still Plucking the grass to know where sits the wind'. This makes for the natural fluidity of speech, avoiding monotony but still maintaining the iambic rhythm.

Date and Text

1596 is the most likely date for *The Merchant of Venice*, for in that year a wealthy Spanish ship was much in the news. The ship had run aground in the harbour at Cadiz, where it was captured and brought to England. It is this event that Salerio is referring to in *Act 1*, Scene 1, lines 25–9:

> I should not see the sandy hour-glass run
> But I should think of shallows and of flats,
> And see my wealthy Andrew dock'd in sand
> Vailing her high-top lower than her ribs
> To kiss her burial.

The earliest text of the play was the Quarto published in 1600, and this is followed in the present edition.

Characters in the play

The Duke of Venice

Antonio	*a merchant of Venice*
Bassanio	*his best friend, in love with Portia*
Gratiano	*another friend, in love with Nerissa*
Lorenzo	*another friend, in love with Jessica*

Salerio
Solanio *other friends*

Leonardo *servant to Bassanio*

Shylock	*a Jew, and a money-lender*
Jessica	*his daughter*
Tubal	*another Jew, Shylock's friend*
Launcelot Gobbo	*servant to Shylock*
Old Gobbo	*Launcelot's father*

Portia *an heiress of Belmont*
Nerissa *her lady-in-waiting*

Prince of Morocco
Prince of Arragon *suitors to Portia*

Balthazar
Stephano *servants to Portia*

Merchants, Officers of the Court of Justice,
Gaoler, Musicians, Servants

Act I

Act I   Scene I

Antonio, the great merchant, is sad, but
he cannot tell his friends the reason for
his sadness. They suggest various
possible causes for anxiety, and try to
make him laugh. Antonio is waiting to
meet his best friend, Bassanio, who
confesses to Antonio that he has spent
a great deal of money, and also that he
is in love with Portia, a rich heiress.
Antonio has no more money to lend
to Bassanio at present, but promises to
help him to borrow from the moneylenders so that he can visit Portia.

1	*In sooth*: truly.
2	*It*: his sadness.
3	*came by*: got.
5	*am to learn*: do not know.
6	*want-wit*: idiot.
7	*ado*: trouble.

Scene I *Venice. A street*

Enter Antonio, Salerio, *and* Solanio

Antonio

In sooth, I know not why I am so sad:
It wearies me; you say it wearies you;
But how I caught it, found it, or came by it,
What stuff 'tis made of, whereof it is born,
5 I am to learn;
And such a want-wit sadness makes of me,
That I have much ado to know myself.

Salerio

Your mind is tossing on the ocean,
There, where your argosies with portly sail,
10 Like signiors and rich burghers on the flood,
Or, as it were, the pageants of the sea,
Do overpeer the petty traffickers,

9   *argosies*: merchant ships.
        portly: stately.
10   *signiors*: gentlemen (the modern
Italian word is *signori*).
        burghers: citizens.
        flood: sea.
11   *pageants*: decorated carts in
carnival processions.
12   *overpeer*: look over the heads of.
        petty traffickers: small commercial
boats.
13   *That . . . reverence*: that bob up
and down, as if they were showing
respect.
15   *had . . . forth*: if I had such
business abroad.
16   *affections*: concerns.
17   *still*: always.
18   *Plucking . . . wind*: holding up a
blade of grass to see in which direction
the wind is blowing.
19   *roads*: harbours.
21   *out of doubt*: without doubt,
certainly.
22   *wind*: breath.
        broth: soup.
23   *ague*: fit of shivering.
25   *sandy hour-glass*. Two spheres of
glass were joined together, with a tiny
hole between them; sand ran from one
sphere to the other, taking just an hour
to do so.
26   *shallows*: shallow waters.
        flats: sandbanks.
27   *Andrew*: a common name for a
big ship at this time; despite the masculine name, the ship—like all English
ships—is referred to as feminine.
        dock'd: run ashore.
28   *Vailing her high-top*: lowering
her mast.
        ribs: the wooden sides of the
ship.
29   *burial*: the sand in which the
ship is being buried.
31   *straight*: immediately.
32   *touching but*: only by touching.
        vessel: both 'ship' and 'con-
tainer'.

That curtsy to them, do them reverence,
As they fly by them with their woven wings.
    Solanio
15 Believe me, sir, had I such venture forth,
The better part of my affections would
Be with my hopes abroad. I should be still
Plucking the grass to know where sits the wind;
Peering in maps for ports, and piers, and roads;
20 And every object that might make me fear
Misfortune to my ventures, out of doubt
Would make me sad.
    Salerio   My wind, cooling my broth,
Would blow me to an ague, when I thought
What harm a wind too great might do at sea.
25 I should not see the sandy hour-glass run
But I should think of shallows and of flats,
And see my wealthy Andrew dock'd in sand
Vailing her high-top lower than her ribs
To kiss her burial. Should I go to church
30 And see the holy edifice of stone,
And not bethink me straight of dangerous rocks,
Which touching but my gentle vessel's side

33-4   *spices . . . silks*: i.e. the cargo.
34   *Enrobe*: clothe.
35   *in a word*: briefly.
35-6   *but . . . nothing*: just a moment ago the cargo was so valuable, and now it is worth nothing.
36-8   *Shall. . . sad*: if I have the imagination to think that this could happen, shall I not also have the imagination to think that, if it happened ('bechanc'd') it would make me sad?
41   *fortune*: both 'luck' and 'wealth'.
42   *ventures*: business.
        bottom: ship.
44   *fortune*: chance.

46   *Fie, fie*: nonsense.

50   *Janus*: a Roman god, always placed above doorways, with one head looking inwards and the other looking out.
51   *fram'd*: constructed.
52   *evermore*: always.
        peep . . . eyes: wrinkle their faces in laughter, so that their eyes appear to be peeping through the folds.
53   *parrots at a bag-piper*. Bagpipes make a dreary noise, and only someone as brainless as a parrot will laugh at it.
54   *vinegar*: bitter.
        aspect: nature.
56   *Nestor*: an old and solemn Greek general, who fought in the Trojan War; a joke must have been very funny if Nestor laughed at it.
57   *kinsman*: probably Solanio means 'friend' and not 'relative'.
62   *regard*: esteem.
63   *calls on*: needs.
64   *embrace th' occasion*: are glad of the chance.

Would scatter all her spices on the stream,
Enrobe the roaring waters with my silks;
35 And, in a word, but even now worth this,
And now worth nothing? Shall I have the thought
To think on this, and shall I lack the thought
That such a thing bechanc'd would make me sad?
But tell not me: I know Antonio
40 Is sad to think upon his merchandise.

    Antonio
Believe me, no: I thank my fortune for it,
My ventures are not in one bottom trusted,
Nor to one place; nor is my whole estate
Upon the fortune of this present year:
45 Therefore, my merchandise makes me not sad.

    Solanio
Why, then you are in love.

    Antonio   Fie, fie!

    Salerio
Not in love neither? Then let us say you are sad
Because you are not merry: and 'twere as easy
For you to laugh and leap, and say you are merry
50 Because you are not sad. Now, by two-headed Janus,
Nature hath fram'd strange fellows in her time:
Some that will evermore peep through their eyes,
And laugh like parrots at a bag-piper;
And other of such vinegar aspect
55 That they'll not show their teeth in way of smile,
Though Nestor swear the jest be laughable.

    Enter Bassanio, Lorenzo, *and* Gratiano

    Solanio
Here comes Bassanio, your most noble kinsman,
Gratiano, and Lorenzo. Fare ye well:
We leave you now with better company.

    Salerio
60 I would have stay'd till I had made you merry,
If worthier friends had not prevented me.

    Antonio
Your worth is very dear in my regard.
I take it, your own business calls on you,
And you embrace th' occasion to depart.

66   *laugh*: meet to enjoy ourselves.
67   *You ... strange*: we don't see you very often.
68   We will have time to spare whenever you do.
71   *have in mind*: remember.
74   You worry about the world too much.
75   Those who spend a lot of time worrying about worldly matters (such as success and happiness) are never really successful or happy.
76   *you ... chang'd*: your appearance has changed a great deal.
77   *hold*: think of.
81   *liver*. The Elizabethans believed that there were four basic character-types—the choleric, the melancholy, the phlegmatic, and the sanguine—and that these types were in part physiologically determined, by the digestion of food in the liver. A liver heated by wine would produce rich blood, and so a lively, sanguine personality.
82   *heart ... groans*. The Elizabethans thought that sighs and groans caused the blood to drain away from the heart.
        mortifying: killing.
84   *like ... alabaster*: like the white stone statue on his grandfather's tomb.
85   *Sleep ... wakes*: be as still and silent during the day as if he were asleep.
        jaundice: a disease that turns the skin yellow; it was thought by the Elizabethans to be associated with jealousy and bad temper (peevishness).
87   *'tis ... speaks*: I am saying this because I love you.
88-9 *whose ... pond*: whose faces are covered in a mask as white and thick as the film on a stagnant pond.
90   *do ... entertain*: deliberately (wilfully) put on an air of solemnity.
91   *With purpose*: in order.
        to be ... opinion: to gain a reputation.
92   *profound conceit*: deep thought.

Salerio
65 Good morrow, my good lords.
      Bassanio
Good signiors both, when shall we laugh? say, when?
You grow exceeding strange: must it be so?
      Salerio
We'll make our leisures to attend on yours.
                              [*Exeunt* Salerio *and* Solanio
    Lorenzo
My Lord Bassanio, since you have found Antonio,
70 We two will leave you; but, at dinner-time,
I pray you, have in mind where we must meet.
    Bassanio
I will not fail you.
    Gratiano
You look not well, Signior Antonio;
You have too much respect upon the world:
75 They lose it that do buy it with much care.
Believe me, you are marvellously chang'd.
      Antonio
I hold the world but as the world, Gratiano;
A stage where every man must play a part,
And mine a sad one.
      Gratiano   Let me play the fool:
80 With mirth and laughter let old wrinkles come,
And let my liver rather heat with wine
Than my heart cool with mortifying groans.
Why should a man, whose blood is warm within,
Sit like his grandsire cut in alabaster,
85 Sleep when he wakes, and creep into the jaundice
By being peevish? I tell thee what, Antonio—
I love thee, and 'tis my love that speaks—
There are a sort of men whose visages
Do cream and mantle like a standing pond,
90 And do a wilful stillness entertain,
With purpose to be dress'd in an opinion
Of wisdom, gravity, profound conceit,

93   *As who should say*: as though he were to say.

      I am Sir Oracle: I speak with the authority of the Greek oracle. The oracle was the voice of the gods, speaking through the mouths of priests.

94   *ope*: open.

96-7   *That . . . nothing*: who have a reputation for being wise only because they never say anything.

98-9   If they were to speak, their listeners would say they were fools, and for saying this the listeners would be damned (because the Bible says that 'whosoever shall say to his brother . . . "Thou fool", shall be in danger of hell fire'; St. Matthew 5: 22).

101-2   Don't try to use this sadness to get such a reputation which is like a silly little fish (not worth having).

104   *exhortation*: sermon.

110   *grow*: become.
      for this gear: because of this nonsense.

112   *a neat's tongue dried*: an ox-tongue, preserved and ready to be eaten.
      a maid not vendible: an old maid (one whom no-one will buy—or marry).

115   *reasons*: thoughts.

117   *ere*: before.

119   *the same*: she.

123   *disabled*: damaged.

124-5   By living in a rather grander style ('port') than my means will permit ('grant continuance').

As who should say, 'I am Sir Oracle,
And when I ope my lips, let no dog bark!'
95 O my Antonio, I do know of these
That therefore only are reputed wise
For saying nothing; when, I am very sure,
If they should speak, would almost damn those ears
Which, hearing them, would call their brothers fools.
100 I'll tell thee more of this another time:
But fish not, with this melancholy bait,
For this fool-gudgeon, this opinion.
Come, good Lorenzo. Fare ye well awhile:
I'll end my exhortation after dinner.
  Lorenzo
105 Well, we will leave you then till dinner-time.
I must be one of these same dumb wise men,
For Gratiano never lets me speak.
  Gratiano
Well, keep me company but two years more,
Thou shalt not know the sound of thine own tongue.
  Antonio
110 Fare you well: I'll grow a talker for this gear.
  Gratiano
Thanks, i' faith; for silence is only commendable
In a neat's tongue dried and a maid not vendible.
      [*Exeunt* Gratiano *and* Lorenzo
  Antonio
Is that anything now?
  Bassanio
Gratiano speaks an infinite deal of nothing, more
115 than any man in all Venice. His reasons are as two grains of wheat hid in two bushels of chaff: you shall seek all day ere you find them, and when you have them, they are not worth the search.
  Antonio
Well, tell me now, what lady is the same
120 To whom you swore a secret pilgrimage,
That you today promis'd to tell me of?
  Bassanio
'Tis not unknown to you, Antonio,
How much I have disabled mine estate,
By something showing a more swelling port

126 *make moan*: complain.
     to be abridg'd: because I have
     been forced to cut down my expenses.
127 *care*: concern.
129 *my time ... prodigal*: my youth,
     which has been rather too lavish;
     Bassanio is comparing himself to the
     Prodigal Son in Christ's parable (St.
     Luke, chapter 15).
130 *gag'd*: in debt.
132-4 Because I know you love me,
     I feel that I have your permission
     ('warranty') to set out before you all my
     plans to free myself from the debts
     I owe.
135 *it*: Bassanio's plan.
136-7 *stand ... Within the eye of
     honour*: looks honourable.
139 *Lie ... occasions*: are all at your
     disposal.
140 *shaft*: arrow.
141 *I ... flight*: I shot an identical
     arrow.
142 *The self-same*: exactly the same.
     more advised watch: watching it
     more carefully.
143 *To ... forth*: to find out the
     other.
     adventuring: risking.
144 *urge*: offer.
     proof: example.
148 *self*: same.
150 *As ... aim*: because I will take
     care ('watch') with what I am doing.
150-1 *or ... Or*: either ... or.
151 *latter hazard*: the second loan
     you have risked.
152 *thankfully rest debtor*: gratefully
     remain in debt to you.
153 *spend but time*: only waste time.
154 To approach my love in such an
     indirect, complicated way.
155 *out of doubt*: indeed.
156 In doubting that I will do every-
     thing I can.
157 *made waste of*: destroyed.
160 *prest unto it*: quite ready to do it.
161 *richly left*: who has inherited
     great wealth.
162 *fairer than that word*: better than
     fair.

125 Than my faint means would grant continuance:
    Nor do I now make moan to be abridg'd
    From such a noble rate; but my chief care
    Is, to come fairly off from the great debts
    Wherein my time, something too prodigal,
130 Hath left me gag'd. To you, Antonio,
    I owe the most, in money and in love;
    And from your love I have a warranty
    To unburden all my plots and purposes
    How to get clear of all the debts I owe.
    Antonio
135 I pray you, good Bassanio, let me know it;
    And if it stand, as you yourself still do,
    Within the eye of honour, be assur'd,
    My purse, my person, my extremest means,
    Lie all unlock'd to your occasions.
    Bassanio
140 In my school-days, when I had lost one shaft,
    I shot his fellow of the self-same flight
    The self-same way with more advised watch,
    To find the other forth; and by adventuring both,
    I oft found both. I urge this childhood proof,
145 Because what follows is pure innocence.
    I owe you much, and (like a wilful youth)
    That which I owe is lost; but if you please
    To shoot another arrow that self way
    Which you did shoot the first, I do not doubt,
150 (As I will watch the aim) or to find both,
    Or bring your latter hazard back again,
    And thankfully rest debtor for the first.
    Antonio
    You know me well, and herein spend but time
    To wind about my love with circumstance;
155 And out of doubt you do me now more wrong
    In making question of my uttermost
    Than if you had made waste of all I have.
    Then do but say to me what I should do
    That in your knowledge may by me be done,
160 And I am prest unto it: therefore speak.
    Bassanio
    In Belmont is a lady richly left,
    And she is fair, and, fairer than that word,
    Of wondrous virtues: sometimes from her eyes

164 *speechless*: unspoken.
165-6 *nothing undervalu'd To*: no less
worthy than.
166 *Portia*: the daughter of a brave
and noble Roman general, Portia was a
tender and loving wife to Brutus (who
led the conspiracy against Julius
Caesar).
169 *locks*: hair.
170 *golden fleece*. In Greek mythology, Jason led an expedition to
Colchis in search of the golden ram's
fleece.
171 *seat*: house.
strand: shore.
172 *quest*: search.
173-4 *had I . . . them*: if I could become
a rival with these suitors.
175 *presages*: prophesies.
thrift: profitable success.
176 *questionless*: without doubt.
177 *fortunes*: wealth.
178 *commodity*: goods, security for a
loan.
179 *a present sum*: cash.
180 See how much you can borrow
in Venice, giving me as your security.
181 *rack'd*: stretched.
182 *furnish thee to Belmont*: provide
what is necessary for you to go to
Belmont.
183 *presently*: at once.
184-5 *I . . . sake*: I have no doubt but
that you will be able to borrow money
either formally on my credit, or for
friendship's sake.

I did receive fair speechless messages:
165 Her name is Portia; nothing undervalu'd
To Cato's daughter, Brutus' Portia;
Nor is the wide world ignorant of her worth,
For the four winds blow in from every coast
Renowned suitors; and her sunny locks
170 Hang on her temples like a golden fleece;
Which makes her seat of Belmont Colchis' strand,
And many Jasons come in quest of her.
O my Antonio, had I but the means
To hold a rival place with one of them,
175 I have a mind presages me such thrift
That I should questionless be fortunate.
    Antonio
Thou know'st that all my fortunes are at sea;
Neither have I money, nor commodity
To raise a present sum: therefore go forth,
180 Try what my credit can in Venice do:
That shall be rack'd, even to the uttermost,
To furnish thee to Belmont, to fair Portia.
Go, presently inquire, and so will I,
Where money is, and I no question make
185 To have it of my trust or for my sake.   [*Exeunt*

Act 1   Scene 2

Portia and Nerissa talk about the test
which Portia's suitors must take. Some
men have already come to Belmont in
the hope of marrying her, but when
Portia describes them she makes fun of
them and shows her dislike. Finally
Nerissa reminds her of Bassanio.

1   *troth*: faith.
         aweary: tired.
4   *in the same abundance*: as
plentiful.
5   *aught*: anything.
         surfeit: eat excessively.
7   *no mean happiness*: no little
happiness.
7–8   *seated in the mean*: placed in the
middle; Nerissa is playing with the two
senses of 'mean'.

Scene 2 *Belmont. A room in Portia's house*

Enter Portia *and* Nerissa

    Portia
By my troth, Nerissa, my little body is aweary of
this great world.
    Nerissa
You would be, sweet madam, if your miseries were
in the same abundance as your good fortunes are:
5 and yet, for aught I see, they are as sick that surfeit
with too much as they that starve with nothing. It is
no mean happiness therefore, to be seated in the
mean: superfluity comes sooner by white hairs, but
competency lives longer.
    Portia
10 Good sentences, and well pronounced.

8-9 Those who have too much (a 'superfluity') grow old quickly, but those who have just enough (a 'competency') live longer.

10 *sentences*: proverbs.
pronounced: spoken. Portia is also hinting at the legal use of 'sentences' which are technically 'pronounced' by judges.

11 *followed*: obeyed.

13 *had been*: would have been.

14 *divine*: preacher.

18 *blood*: will. Portia is making the distinction between reason and will, or mind and body.

19-20 Youthful high spirits are like a hare, which easily leaps over the nets ('meshes') of limping good advice.

21 *reasoning*: wise talk.
in the fashion: the right way.

22 *O me*: oh dear.

23 *I would*: I like.

24 *the will*: Portia plays with the two meanings, 'desire' and 'testament'.
curbed: restrained.

27 *ever*: always.

30-1 *his meaning*: the one that Portia's father meant him to choose.

32 *rightly*: Nerissa plays with the two meanings, 'correctly' and 'truly'.

36 *over-name them*: call out their names.

38 *level*: guess.

39-98 For an explanation of the comedy of these lines, see Introduction, p. xii.

39 *Neapolitan*: from Naples.

40 *colt*: awkward young man (like a young horse).

41-2 *a great . . . parts*: point in his own favour.

43 *afeard*: afraid.

44 *smith*: blacksmith.

45 *County Palatine*: a count who reigned over territory which in other countries would be ruled by a king.

Nerissa
They would be better if well followed.

Portia
If to do were as easy as to know what were good to do, chapels had been churches, and poor men's cottages princes' palaces. It is a good divine that
15 follows his own instructions: I can easier teach twenty what were good to be done, than be one of the twenty to follow mine own teaching. The brain may devise laws for the blood, but a hot temper leaps o'er a cold decree: such a hare is madness (the youth),
20 to skip o'er the meshes of good counsel (the cripple). But this reasoning is not in the fashion to choose me a husband. O me, the word 'choose'! I may neither choose who I would nor refuse who I dislike; so is the will of a living daughter curbed by the will of
25 a dead father. Is it not hard, Nerissa, that I cannot choose one, nor refuse none?

Nerissa
Your father was ever virtuous, and holy men at their death have good inspirations; therefore, the lottery that he hath devised in these three chests of
30 gold, silver, and lead, whereof who chooses his meaning chooses you, will, no doubt, never be chosen by any rightly but one who you shall rightly love. But what warmth is there in your affection towards any of these princely suitors that are
35 already come?

Portia
I pray thee, over-name them, and as thou namest them, I will describe them; and, according to my description, level at my affection.

Nerissa
First there is the Neapolitan prince.

Portia
40 Ay, that's a colt indeed, for he doth nothing but talk of his horse, and he makes it a great appropriation to his own good parts that he can shoe him himself. I am much afeard my lady his mother played false with a smith.

Nerissa
45 Then is there the County Palatine.

46   *as who should say*: as if he were to say.
47   *choose*: pick anyone you will.
48   *prove*: become like.
48-9 *the weeping philosopher*: Heraclitus of Ephesus, who went to live alone in the mountains because he was so distressed by mankind's stupidity.
50   *unmannerly*: rude.
51   *death's-head*: skull.

54   *How say you by*: what do you think of?

56   *pass for*: be accepted as.
57   *to be mocker*: to mock at.

60   *he is . . . no man*: he has everybody else's characteristics and no personality of his own.
61   *throstle*: thrush.
      falls straight a-capering: immediately starts jumping up and down (to the music).

70   *come into court*: bear witness.
71   *poor pennyworth*: not very much (as much as could be bought for a penny).
72   *proper man's picture*: the appearance of a handsome man.
73   *a dumb-show*: a mime, acting without words.
74   *suited*: dressed.
      doublet: tunic.
75   *round hose*: breeches.
76   *behaviour*: manners.
79   *borrowed . . . of*: received . . . from.
      a box of the ear: a blow on the ear.
81   *became his surety*: guaranteed that he would repay the debt.
      sealed under: signed his name underneath the Scotsman's signature on the (imaginary) bond.

Portia
He doth nothing but frown, as who should say, 'And you will not have me, choose.' He hears merry tales, and smiles not: I fear he will prove the weeping philosopher when he grows old, being so full of
50 unmannerly sadness in his youth. I had rather be married to a death's-head with a bone in his mouth than to either of these. God defend me from these two!

Nerissa
How say you by the French lord, Monsieur Le
55 Bon?

Portia
God made him, and therefore let him pass for a man. In truth, I know it is a sin to be mocker; but, he! why, he hath a horse better than the Neapolitan's, a better bad habit of frowning than
60 the Count Palatine; he is every man in no man; if a throstle sing, he falls straight a-capering; he will fence with his own shadow. If I should marry him, I should marry twenty husbands: if he would despise me, I would forgive him, for if he loves
65 me to madness, I shall never requite him.

Nerissa
What say you, then, to Falconbridge, the young baron of England?

Portia
You know I say nothing to him, for he understands not me, nor I him: he hath neither Latin, French,
70 nor Italian; and you will come into the court and swear that I have a poor pennyworth in the English. He is a proper man's picture, but, alas! who can converse with a dumb-show? How oddly he is suited! I think he bought his doublet in Italy, his
75 round hose in France, his bonnet in Germany, and his behaviour everywhere.

Nerissa
What think you of the Scottish lord, his neighbour?

Portia
That he hath a neighbourly charity in him, for he borrowed a box of the ear of the Englishman, and
80 swore he would pay him again when he was able: I think the Frenchman became his surety and sealed under for another.

Nerissa

How like you the young German, the Duke of
Saxony's nephew?

Portia

85 Very vilely in the morning, when he is sober, and
most vilely in the afternoon, when he is drunk:
when he is best, he is a little worse than a man, and
when he is worst, he is little better than a beast. And
the worst fall that ever fell, I hope I shall make shift
90 to go without him.

Nerissa

If he should offer to choose, and choose the right
casket, you should refuse to perform your father's
will, if you should refuse to accept him.

Portia

Therefore, for fear of the worst, I pray thee, set a
95 deep glass of Rhenish wine on the contrary casket,
for, if the devil be within and that temptation without, I know he will choose it. I will do anything,
Nerissa, ere I will be married to a sponge.

Nerissa

You need not fear, lady, the having any of these
100 lords: they have acquainted me with their determinations; which is, indeed, to return to their home
and to trouble you with no more suit, unless you
may be won by some other sort than your father's
imposition depending on the caskets.

Portia

105 If I live to be as old as Sibylla, I will die as chaste
as Diana, unless I be obtained by the manner of my
father's will. I am glad this parcel of wooers are so
reasonable, for there is not one among them but I
dote on his very absence, and I pray God grant
110 them a fair departure.

Nerissa

Do you not remember, lady, in your father's time,
a Venetian, a scholar and a soldier, that came hither
in company of the Marquis of Montferrat?

Portia

Yes, yes: it was Bassanio—as I think so was he
115 called.

88-9   *And . . . fell*: if ('And') the
worst that ever happened ('fell') should
happen ('fall').

89   *make shift*: manage.

91   *offer*: decide.

95   *Rhenish wine*: German white
wine, from the district of the Rhine.
contrary: other.

99   *the having*: that you will have to
accept.
100   *acquainted me with*: informed me
of.
determinations: decisions.
103   *sort*: way.

105   *Sibylla*: the Sibyl of Cumae, a
prophetess in classical mythology;
Apollo granted her as many years of
life as the number of grains of sand that
she held in her hand.
106   *Diana*: the goddess of virginity
in classical mythology.
107   *parcel*: set.

True, madam: he of all the men that ever my foolish
eyes looked upon, was the best deserving a fair
lady.

Portia

I remember him well, and I remember him worthy
120 of thy praise.

Enter a Servant

How now, what news?

Servant

The four strangers seek for you, madam, to take
their leave; and there is a forerunner come from a
fifth, the Prince of Morocco, who brings word the
125 prince his master will be here tonight.

Portia

If I could bid the fifth welcome with so good heart
as I can bid the other four farewell, I should be glad
of his approach: if he have the condition of a saint
and the complexion of a devil, I had rather he
130 should shrive me than wive me.
Come, Nerissa. [*To Attendant*] Sirrah, go before.
Whiles we shut the gate upon one wooer, another
    knocks at the door.   [*Exeunt*

Scene 3 *Venice. A public place*

Enter Bassanio *and* Shylock

Shylock

Three thousand ducats; well.

Bassanio

Ay, sir, for three months.

Shylock

For three months; well.

Bassanio

For the which, as I told you, Antonio shall be
5 bound.

Shylock

Antonio shall become bound; well.

122   *four.* Shakespeare seems to have
forgotten that six suitors have been
discussed.

123   *fore-runner*: messenger who came
ahead of his master, herald.

128   *condition*: nature.
129   *complexion*: appearance.
130   *shrive me*: hear my confession
and give absolutions—as a holy man or
'saint' would.
    wive me: make me his wife.

Act 1   Scene 3
Shylock is able to lend money to
Bassanio, but he makes it clear that he
hates Antonio. Shylock and Antonio
argue about the morality of making a
profit from money-lending, and
Shylock reminds Antonio of his past
insults. However, he agrees to lend the
money; but he asks for an unusual
bond.

1   *ducats*: Venetian gold coins.

5   *bound*: as security.

7   *stead*: supply.

16   *sufficient*: financially adequate.
are in supposition: have to be
taken on trust (because his property is
all outside Venice, as Shylock goes on
to explain).

17   *argosy*: merchant ship.
18   *the Rialto*: the Venetian Stock
Exchange; the name is often used
today for the bridge leading to the
Exchange.

20   *squandered*: scattered lavishly.

30   *pork*: meat forbidden to the
Jews.
30-1 *the habitation . . . into*: Jesus
('the Nazarite') healed a madman by
ordering the devils that possessed his
mind to leave the man and enter into
a herd of pigs (St. Mark 5: 1-13).
33   *and so following*: etc.

37   *fawning*: servile.
publican: innkeeper.
38   *for*: because.

Bassanio

May you stead me? Will you pleasure me? Shall
I know your answer?

Shylock

Three thousand ducats, for three months, and
10 Antonio bound.

Bassanio

Your answer to that?

Shylock

Antonio is a good man.

Bassanio

Have you heard any imputation to the contrary?

Shylock

Ho, no, no, no, no; my meaning in saying he is
15 a good man is to have you understand me that he is
sufficient. Yet his means are in supposition: he hath
an argosy bound to Tripolis, another to the Indies;
I understand moreover, upon the Rialto, he hath
a third at Mexico, a fourth for England, and other
20 ventures he hath squandered abroad. But ships are
but boards, sailors but men: there be land-rats and
water-rats, water-thieves and land-thieves—I mean
pirates—and then there is the peril of waters, winds,
and rocks. The man is, notwithstanding, sufficient.
25 Three thousand ducats; I think I may take his bond.

Bassanio

Be assured you may.

Shylock

I will be assured I may; and, that I may be assured,
I will bethink me. May I speak with Antonio?

Bassanio

If it please you to dine with us.

Shylock

30 Yes, to smell pork; to eat of the habitation which
your prophet the Nazarite conjured the devil into.
I will buy with you, sell with you, talk with you,
walk with you, and so following; but I will not eat
with you, drink with you, nor pray with you. What
35 news on the Rialto? Who is he comes here?

Enter Antonio

Bassanio

This is Signior Antonio

Shylock

[*Aside*] How like a fawning publican he looks!
I hate him for he is a Christian;

39   *low*: base.
      simplicity: foolishness.
40   *gratis*: free of interest.
41   *usance*: usury, money-lending.
42   *upon the hip*: off his guard, at
a disadvantage.
43   *feed fat*: i.e. as though the grudge
were an animal to be looked after.
44   *rails*: abuses.
46   *thrift*: success.
47   *interest*: profit.

49   *debating of*: reckoning up.
      present store: ready money.
50   *near*: close.
51   *gross*: whole sum.

54   *furnish*: supply.
      soft: wait a minute.

56   *in our mouths*: that we were
talking about.

57   *albeit*: although.
58   *excess*: interest (an amount
exceeding the original sum lent or
borrowed).
59   *ripe*: urgent.
60   *possess'd*: informed.
61   *would*: want.

66   *Upon advantage*: with interest.
      I do never use it: I have never
done it.
67-84   There are two stories about
Jacob in the Book of Genesis. The first
(chapters 25 and 27) tell how, with the
aid of 'his wise mother', he tricked his
elder brother of his birth-right, and so
became the heir to his father and to his
grandfather, Abraham, the founder of
the Jewish race. The second story
(chapter 30) tells of Jacob's cunning
trick with Laban's sheep; Shylock
recounts this episode.
67   *graz'd*: shepherded.
69   *wrought*: devised.

But more for that in low simplicity
40 He lends out money gratis, and brings down
The rate of usance here with us in Venice.
If I can catch him once upon the hip,
I will feed fat the ancient grudge I bear him.
He hates our sacred nation, and he rails,
45 Even there where merchants most do congregate,
On me, my bargains, and my well-won thrift,
Which he calls interest. Cursed be my tribe,
If I forgive him!
    Bassanio   Shylock, do you hear?
    Shylock
I am debating of my present store,
50 And, by the near guess of my memory,
I cannot instantly raise up the gross
Of full three thousand ducats. What of that?
Tubal, a wealthy Hebrew of my tribe,
Will furnish me. But soft! how many months
55 Do you desire? [*To* Antonio] Rest you fair, good
    signior;
Your worship was the last man in our mouths.
    Antonio
Shylock, albeit I neither lend nor borrow
By taking nor by giving of excess,
Yet, to supply the ripe wants of my friend,
60 I'll break a custom. [*To* Bassanio] Is he yet possess'd
How much ye would?
    Shylock   Ay, ay, three thousand ducats.
    Antonio
And for three months.
    Shylock
I had forgot; three months; you told me so.
Well then, your bond; and let me see—but hear you;
65 Methought you said, you neither lend nor borrow
Upon advantage.
    Antonio   I do never use it.
    Shylock
When Jacob graz'd his uncle Laban's sheep—
This Jacob from our holy Abram was,
As his wise mother wrought in his behalf,
70 The third possessor: ay, he was the third—
    Antonio
And what of him? did he take interest?

74   *compromis'd*: agreed.
75   *eanlings*: new-born lambs.
      streak'd and pied: with fleeces of
two colours.
76   *fall as Jacob's hire*: be counted
as Jacob's wages.
      rank: on heat, ready for mating.
80   *pill'd . . . wands*: peeled the bark
from some twigs (so that they appeared
to be striped).
81   *deed of kind*: act of breeding.
82   *fulsome*: passionate.
83   *eaning*: lambing.
84   *Fall*: give birth to.
86   *thrift*: profit.

87   *venture*: enterprise.
      serv'd for: was a servant for.
88   *sway'd*: ruled.
      fashion'd: shaped.
90   Did you introduce this story as
a justification of usury?

94   *cite*: quote.

101   *beholding*: indebted.

102   *oft*: often.
103   *rated*: scolded.
104   *usances*: financial deals.
105   *Still*: always.
106   *sufferance*: long-suffering.
      badge: characteristic.

Shylock
No, not take interest; not, as you would say,
Directly interest: mark what Jacob did.
When Laban and himself were compromis'd,
75   That all the eanlings which were streak'd and pied
Should fall as Jacob's hire, the ewes, being rank,
In end of autumn turned to the rams;
And, when the work of generation was
Between these woolly breeders in the act,
80   The skilful shepherd pill'd me certain wands,
And, in the doing of the deed of kind,
He stuck them up before the fulsome ewes,
Who, then conceiving, did in eaning time
Fall parti-colour'd lambs, and those were Jacob's.
85   This was a way to thrive, and he was blest:
And thrift is blessing, if men steal it not.
     Antonio
This was a venture, sir, that Jacob serv'd for;
A thing not in his power to bring to pass,
But sway'd and fashion'd by the hand of heaven.
90   Was this inserted to make interest good?
Or is your gold and silver ewes and rams?
     Shylock
I cannot tell; I make it breed as fast:
But note me, signior.—
     Antonio   Mark you this, Bassanio,
The devil can cite Scripture for his purpose.
95   An evil soul, producing holy witness,
Is like a villain with a smiling cheek,
A goodly apple rotten at the heart.
O what a goodly outside falsehood hath!
     Shylock
Three thousand ducats; 'tis a good round sum.
100 Three months from twelve: then, let me see, the
        rate—
     Antonio
Well, Shylock, shall we be beholding to you?
     Shylock
Signior Antonio, many a time and oft
In the Rialto you have rated me
About my moneys and my usances:
105 Still have I borne it with a patient shrug,
For sufferance is the badge of all our tribe.

107   *misbeliever*: heretic, unbeliever.
108   *gaberdine*: long loose coat, worn traditionally by Jews.

111   *Go to, then*: and now what are you doing (an expression of exasperation).
112   *moneys*. The plural form may be Shakespeare's attempt to indicate some Jewish speech habit.
113   *void your rheum*: spit.
114   *foot*: kick.
115   *suit*: request.

119   *key*: tone.
120   *With bated breath*: anxiously.

126   *as like*: just as likely.

130   *A breed . . . metal*: a product of sterile metal.
132   *break*: fail to keep his bond.

136   *doit*: jot (a very small amount).
137   *usance*: interest.
138   *kind*: kindness; but see Introduction, p. xiv.

140   *notary*: solicitor.
       seal me: sign for me.
141   *single*: simple.
       in a merry sport: as a joke.
144   *Express'd in the condition*: set down in the formal agreement.
145   *nominated for*: named as.
       equal: accurate.

You call me misbeliever, cut-throat dog,
And spit upon my Jewish gaberdine,
And all for use of that which is mine own.
110 Well then, it now appears you need my help:
Go to then; you come to me, and you say,
'Shylock, we would have moneys:' you say so;
You, that did void your rheum upon my beard,
And foot me as you spurn a stranger cur
115 Over your threshold. Moneys is your suit.
What should I say to you? Should I not say,
'Hath a dog money? Is it possible
A cur can lend three thousand ducats?' or
Shall I bend low, and in a bondman's key,
120 With bated breath, and whispering humbleness,
Say this:
'Fair sir, you spat on me on Wednesday last;
You spurn'd me such a day; another time
You call'd me dog—and for these courtesies
125 I'll lend you thus much moneys'?

Antonio
I am as like to call thee so again,
To spit on thee again, to spurn thee too.
If thou wilt lend this money, lend it not
As to thy friends, for when did friendship take
130 A breed for barren metal of his friend?
But lend it rather to thine enemy;
Who if he break, thou may'st with better face
Exact the penalty.

Shylock   Why, look you, how you storm!
I would be friends with you, and have your love,
135 Forget the shames that you have stain'd me with,
Supply your present wants, and take no doit
Of usance for my moneys, and you'll not hear me:
This is kind I offer.

Bassanio
This were kindness.

Shylock   This kindness will I show.
140 Go with me to a notary, seal me there
Your single bond; and, in a merry sport,
If you repay me not on such a day,
In such a place, such sum or sums as are
Express'd in the condition, let the forfeit
145 Be nominated for an equal pound

Of your fair flesh, to be cut off and taken
In what part of your body pleaseth me.

Antonio

Content, in faith: I'll seal to such a bond,
And say there is much kindness in the Jew.

Bassanio

150 You shall not seal to such a bond for me:
I'll rather dwell in my necessity.

151   *dwell*: remain.

Antonio

Why, fear not, man, I will not forfeit it:
Within these two months, that's a month before
This bond expires, I do expect return
155 Of thrice three times the value of this bond.

Shylock

O father Abram, what these Christians are,
Whose own hard dealings teaches them suspect
The thoughts of others! Pray you, tell me this:
If he should break his day, what should I gain
160 By the exaction of the forfeiture?
A pound of man's flesh, taken from a man,
Is not so estimable, profitable neither,
As flesh of muttons, beefs, or goats. I say,
To buy his favour, I extend this friendship:
165 If he will take it, so; if not, adieu;
And, for my love, I pray you wrong me not.

157   *hard*: tough.
       suspect: be suspicious of.

159   *break his day*: fail to pay on the
       agreed date.

Antonio

Yes, Shylock, I will seal unto this bond.

Shylock

Then meet me forthwith at the notary's;
Give him direction for this merry bond.
170 And I will go and purse the ducats straight,
See to my house, left in the fearful guard
Of an unthrifty knave, and presently
I'll be with you.   [*Exit* Shylock

170   *purse the ducats*: put the ducats
       in a purse.
171   *fearful*: not to be trusted.
172   *unthrifty*: careless.
       knave: lad, servant.

Antonio   Hie thee, gentle Jew.
The Hebrew will turn Christian: he grows kind.

Bassanio

175 I like not fair terms and a villain's mind.

Antonio

Come on: in this there can be no dismay;
My ships come home a month before the day.

                                        [*Exeunt*

Act 2

Act 2   Scene 1
Portia meets the Prince of Morocco,
who wants to marry her; he chooses to
try his luck with the caskets, although
she warns him of the penalty he must
pay if he makes the wrong choice.

1   *Mislike*: dislike.
2   *shadow'd*: dark.
       livery: uniform.
3   *near bred*: closely related.
4   *fairest*: both 'most handsome'
and 'with the palest skin'.
5   *Phœbus*: the classical sun-god.
6   And let us [himself and the fair
northern prince] cut ourselves for love
of you.
7   *whose blood is reddest*: the
Elizabethans believed that red blood
was a sign of good spirits and courage;
see note to 1, 1, 80.
8   *aspect*: appearance.
9   *fear'd*: frightened.
10   *regarded*: esteemed.
       clime: climate, country.
11   *hue*: colour.
12   *steal your thoughts*: win your
affections.
13   *In terms of choice*: in the matter
of choosing.
13-14   *I am . . . eyes*: I am not in-
fluenced only by what my eyes (which
are not easy to please—'nice') tell me
to do.
15   *the lottery of my destiny*: the fact
that my fate depends upon luck.

Scene 1 *Belmont. A room in Portia's house*

Enter the Prince of Morocco, *and his*
Followers; Portia *and* Nerissa

Morocco
Mislike me not for my complexion,
The shadow'd livery of the burnish'd sun,
To whom I am a neighbour, and near bred.
Bring me the fairest creature northward born,
5 Where Phœbus' fire scarce thaws the icicles,
And let us make incision for your love,
To prove whose blood is reddest, his or mine.
I tell thee, lady, this aspect of mine
Hath fear'd the valiant: by my love, I swear
10 The best regarded virgins of our clime
Have lov'd it too: I would not change this hue,
Except to steal your thoughts, my gentle queen.

Portia
In terms of choice I am not solely led
By nice direction of a maiden's eyes;
15 Besides, the lottery of my destiny
Bars me the right of voluntary choosing:
But if my father had not scanted me
And hedg'd me by his wit, to yield myself
His wife who wins me by that means I told you,
20 Yourself, renowned prince, then stood as fair
As any comer I have look'd on yet
For my affection.
          Morocco   Even for that I thank you:
Therefore, I pray you, lead me to the caskets

16   *Bars*: forbids.
       voluntary choosing: choosing
what I want.
17   *scanted*: restricted.
18   *hedg'd me*: bound me in.
       wit: wisdom.
18–19 *to yield myself His wife*: to give
myself as a wife to that man.
20   *stood as fair*: had as good a
chance (with, also, a play on 'fair' =
fair-skinned).
21   *any comer*: anyone who has
come.
24   *scimitar*: short, curved sword.
25   *Sophy*: Emperor of Persia.
26   *of*: from.
       Sultan Solyman: leader of the
Turks against the Persians in 1535.
27   *o'erstare*: outface, defy.
31   *alas the while*: Morocco sighs.
32   *Hercules and Lichas*: Hercules
was the super-man of classical mythology and Lichas was his servant.
33   *Which . . . man*: to find out
which is the better man.
35   *Alcides*: another name for
Hercules, meaning 'son of Alcaeus'.
42   *In way of*: on the subject of.
       advis'd: warned.
43   *Nor will not*: I will not ask anyone else to marry me.
       chance: fate, trial.
44   *forward*: let us go forward.
45   *hazard*: gamble.
46   *cursed'st*: most cursed.

Act 2   Scene 2
Launcelot Gobbo, Shylock's servant, is
wondering whether he ought to run
away from his master. Old Gobbo, his
father, comes on to the stage in search
of his son; because he is blind he does
not recognize Launcelot, who plays a
rather cruel trick on him. Old Gobbo
asks Bassanio to give employment to
Launcelot, which Bassanio agrees to do.
Gratiano also asks a favour from
Bassanio: he wants to accompany him
to Belmont. Bassanio agrees, but he
warns Gratiano that he must behave
properly.

To try my fortune. By this scimitar—
25 That slew the Sophy, and a Persian prince
That won three fields of Sultan Solyman—
I would o'erstare the sternest eyes that look;
Outbrave the heart most daring on the earth;
Pluck the young sucking cubs from the she-bear;
30 Yea, mock the lion when he roars for prey,
To win thee, lady. But, alas the while!
If Hercules and Lichas play at dice
Which is the better man, the greater throw
May turn by fortune from the weaker hand:
35 So is Alcides beaten by his page;
And so may I, blind fortune leading me,
Miss that which one unworthier may attain,
And die with grieving.
       Portia   You must take your chance;
And either not attempt to choose at all,
40 Or swear before you choose, if you choose wrong,
Never to speak to lady afterward
In way of marriage: therefore be advis'd.
       Morocco
Nor will not: come, bring me unto my chance.
       Portia
First, forward to the temple: after dinner
45 Your hazard shall be made.
       Morocco   Good fortune then!
To make me blest or cursed'st among men!
                                        [*Exeunt*

Scene 2 *Venice. The street outside Shylock's house*

Enter Launcelot Gobbo
       Launcelot
Certainly my conscience will serve me to run from
this Jew my master. The fiend is at mine elbow,
and tempts me, saying to me, 'Gobbo, Launcelot
Gobbo, good Launcelot,' or 'good Gobbo,' or 'good
5 Launcelot Gobbo, use your legs, take the start, run
away.' My conscience says, 'No; take heed, honest
Launcelot; take heed, honest Gobbo;' or, as afore-
said, 'honest Launcelot Gobbo; do not run; scorn
running with thy heels.' Well, the most courageous

1   *serve*: assist.

6   *heed*: care.

8–9   *scorn . . . heels*: both 'be utterly contemptuous of running' and 'be contemptuous of using your legs to run away'.

10   *pack*: hurry off.
     Via: on your way (Latin).

11   *for the heavens*: for heaven's sake.
     rouse up: awaken.

13   *hanging . . . heart*: clinging to my heart (like a wife with her arms round his neck).

15–16   *honest woman*: virtuous woman.

16–17   *my father . . . grow to*: Launcelot hints, without completing the suggestion, that his father enjoyed the company of women other than his wife.

18   *budge*: move.

23   *God bless the mark*: a phrase meaning, roughly, 'if I may say so'.

25   *saving your reverence*: a phrase meaning, roughly, 'with all due respect'. Launcelot is apologizing to the audience for using such strong language ('the devil').

27   *incarnation*: Launcelot's error for 'incarnate' (= in the flesh).
     in my conscience: to speak truly.

28   *hard*: strict.

34   *true-begotten father*: a joke, because it is the father who begets the son.

35   *sand-blind*: half-blind.
     high gravel-blind: almost completely blind (which would be 'stone-blind').

36   *try confusions*: try out a test on him.

40   *marry*: by the Virgin Mary (a mild oath).

10 fiend bids me pack: '*Via!*' says the fiend; 'away!' says the fiend; 'for the heavens, rouse up a brave mind,' says the fiend, 'and run.' Well, my conscience, hanging about the neck of my heart, says very wisely to me, 'My honest friend Launcelot,

15 being an honest man's son,'—or rather an honest woman's son, for, indeed, my father did something smack, something grow to, he had a kind of taste—well, my conscience says, 'Launcelot, budge not.' 'Budge!' says the fiend. 'Budge not!' says my

20 conscience. 'Conscience,' say I, 'you counsel well;' 'Fiend,' say I, 'you counsel well.' To be ruled by my conscience, I should stay with the Jew my master, who (God bless the mark!) is a kind of devil; and, to run away from the Jew, I should be ruled

25 by the fiend, who (saving your reverence) is the devil himself. Certainly, the Jew is the very devil incarnation; and, in my conscience, my conscience is but a kind of hard conscience, to offer to counsel me to stay with the Jew. The fiend gives the more

30 friendly counsel: I will run, fiend; my heels are at your commandment; I will run.

Enter Old Gobbo, *with a basket*

Gobbo

Master young man, you; I pray you, which is the way to Master Jew's?

Launcelot

[*Aside*] O heavens! this is my true-begotten father,

35 who, being more than sand-blind, high gravel-blind, knows me not: I will try confusions with him.

Gobbo

Master young gentleman, I pray you, which is the way to Master Jew's?

Launcelot

Turn up on your right hand at the next turning,

40 but, at the next turning of all, on your left; marry, at the very next turning, turn of no hand, but turn down indirectly to the Jew's house.

43   *sonties*: saints (Old Gobbo speaks a country dialect).
      hit: find.
44   *one Launcelot*: a certain Launcelot.

47   *raise the waters*: bring tears to his eyes.

51   *well to live*: in good health.

52   *'a*: he.

55   *ergo*: Latin for 'therefore'—but Launcelot does not know the meaning, and uses the word merely to bewilder the old man.
57   *an 't*: if it.
      mastership: Gobbo invents the word, as being suitable for one who so insists on calling Launcelot 'master' (compare 'lordship' and 'ladyship').
59   *father*: a common way of addressing an old man; Launcelot uses it for comedy.
61   *the sisters three*: the Fates, three goddesses in classical mythology who controlled human destiny.

66   *hovel-post*: main timber supporting a poor dwelling.

68   *Alack the day*: Old Gobbo groans.

Gobbo
By God's sonties, 'twill be a hard way to hit. Can you tell me whether one Launcelot, that dwells with
45 him, dwell with him or no?
Launcelot
Talk you of young Master Launcelot? [*Aside*] Mark me now; now will I raise the waters. Talk you of young Master Launcelot?
Gobbo
No 'master', sir, but a poor man's son; his father,
50 though I say 't, is an honest, exceeding poor man, and, God be thanked, well to live.
Launcelot
Well, let his father be what 'a will, we talk of young Master Launcelot.
Gobbo
Your worship's friend, and Launcelot, sir.
Launcelot
55 But I pray you, *ergo*, old man, *ergo*, I beseech you, talk you of young Master Launcelot?
Gobbo
Of Launcelot, an 't please your mastership.
Launcelot
Ergo, Master Launcelot. Talk not of Master Launcelot, father; for the young gentleman (accord-
60 ing to fates and destinies and such odd sayings, the sisters three and such branches of learning) is, indeed, deceased; or, as you would say in plain terms, gone to heaven.
Gobbo
Marry, God forbid! the boy was the very staff of
65 my age, my very prop.
Launcelot
[*Aside*] Do I look like a cudgel or a hovel-post, a staff or a prop? Do you know me, father?
Gobbo
Alack the day! I know you not, young gentleman: but I pray you, tell me, is my boy—God rest his
70 soul!—alive or dead?

74-5   *it is . . . child*: Launcelot inverts the proverb 'it is a wise child that knows his own father'.

78   *out*: come out.

Launcelot

Do you not know me, father?

Gobbo

Alack, sir, I am sand-blind; I know you not.

Launcelot

Nay, indeed, if you had your eyes, you might fail
of the knowing me: it is a wise father that knows his
75 own child. Well, old man, I will tell you news of
your son. [*Kneels*] Give me your blessing: truth
will come to light; murder cannot be hid long;
a man's son may, but, in the end, truth will out.

Gobbo

Pray you, sir, stand up. I am sure you are not
80 Launcelot, my boy.

Launcelot

Pray you, let's have no more fooling about it, but
give me your blessing: I am Launcelot, your boy
that was, your son that is, your child that shall be.

Gobbo

I cannot think you are my son.

Launcelot

85 I know not what I shall think of that; but I am
Launcelot, the Jew's man, and I am sure Margery
your wife is my mother.

Gobbo

Her name is Margery, indeed: I'll be sworn, if thou
be Launcelot, thou art mine own flesh and blood.

90   *Lord . . . be*: the Lord be praised.

92   *fill-horse*: cart-horse (one that works in the 'fills' or shafts).

93   *backward*: i.e. shorter.

94   *of*: on.

90 Lord worshipped might he be! what a beard hast
thou got! thou hast got more hair on thy chin than
Dobbin my fill-horse has on his tail.

Launcelot

It should seem then that Dobbin's tail grows backward: I am sure he had more hair of his tail than
95 I have of my face, when I last saw him.

Gobbo

Lord, how art thou changed! How dost thou and
thy master agree? I have brought him a present.
How 'gree you now?

97   *agree*: suit each other.

98   *'gree*: agree.

99   *for mine own part*: as far as I am
concerned.

99-100   *set up my rest*: made up my
mind.

101   *ground*: distance.

102   *halter*: i.e. a rope to hang himself with.

103   *tell*: count.

103-4   *finger . . . ribs*: another of
Launcelot's reversals; perhaps he
spreads his own hand over his chest,
and runs his father's hand across the
fingers as though they were his ribs.

104-5   *give me your present*: just give
your present.

106   *liveries*: uniforms, jobs.

110   *hasted*: speeded up.

112   *put . . . making*: arrange for the
uniforms to be made.

113   *anon*: at once.

114   *To him*: speak to him.

116   *Gramercy*: many thanks (from
the French *grand merci*).

120   *infection*: Gobbo's mistake for
'affection' = desire.

122   *the short and the long*: all that
needs to be said (the more usual idiom
is 'the long and the short').

Launcelot

Well, well: but, for mine own part, as I have set
100 up my rest to run away, so I will not rest till I have
run some ground. My master's a very Jew: give him
a present? give him a halter! I am famished in his
service; you may tell every finger I have with my
ribs. Father, I am glad you are come: give me your
105 present to one Master Bassanio, who, indeed, gives
rare new liveries. If I serve not him, I will run as
far as God has any ground. O rare fortune! here
comes the man: to him, father; for I am a Jew, if
I serve the Jew any longer.

Enter Bassanio, *with* Leonardo, *and other*
Servants

Bassanio

110 You may do so; but let it be so hasted that supper
be ready at the farthest by five of the clock. See
these letters delivered; put the liveries to making;
and desire Gratiano to come anon to my lodging.

[*Exit a* Servant

Launcelot

To him, father.

Gobbo

115 God bless your worship!

Bassanio

Gramercy! wouldst thou aught with me?

Gobbo

Here's my son, sir, a poor boy—

Launcelot

Not a poor boy, sir, but the rich Jew's man; that
would, sir—as my father shall specify—

Gobbo

120 He hath a great infection, sir (as one would say) to
serve—

Launcelot

Indeed, the short and the long is, I serve the Jew,
and have a desire, as my father shall specify—

124   *saving . . . reverence*: with respect to you, sir (an apology for the dialect expression that he is going to use).

125   *cater-cousins*: good friends (fellow bread-eaters).

128   *frutify*: fructify (bear fruit); Launcelot really means 'notify'.

129   *dish of doves*: doves ready for eating; the gift is a kind of bribe to persuade Bassanio to grant his request ('suit').

131   *impertinent*: impudent—the very opposite of what Launcelot means to say, which is 'pertinent' (= relevant).

137   *defect*: Old Gobbo means to say 'effect' (= conclusion).

138   *thou . . . suit*: your request is granted.

140   *preferr'd*: recommended.
       preferment: promotion.

143   *The old proverb*: the proverb is 'The grace of God is gear enough', meaning that the man who has the grace of God has all he needs for salvation. As a Christian, Bassanio should have 'the grace of God', and as a rich man, Shylock has 'enough'.
       parted: divided.

147-8 *inquire . . . out*: make your way to my house.

149   *More . . . fellows*: with more gold braid on it than the uniforms of the other servants, his mates. The additional decoration might indicate that Launcelot is to be Bassanio's jester.

Gobbo
His master and he (saving your worship's reverence)
125 are scarce cater-cousins.

   Launcelot
To be brief, the very truth is that the Jew having
done me wrong, doth cause me—as my father,
being, I hope, an old man, shall frutify unto you—

   Gobbo
I have here a dish of doves that I would bestow
130 upon your worship, and my suit is—

   Launcelot
In very brief, the suit is impertinent to myself, as
your worship shall know by this honest old man;
and, though I say it, though old man, yet (poor
man) my father.

   Bassanio
135 One speak for both. What would you?

   Launcelot
Serve you, sir.

   Gobbo
That is the very defect of the matter, sir.

   Bassanio
I know thee well; thou hast obtain'd thy suit:
Shylock thy master spoke with me this day,
140 And hath preferr'd thee, if it be preferment
To leave a rich Jew's service, to become
The follower of so poor a gentleman.

   Launcelot
The old proverb is very well parted between my
master Shylock and you, sir: you have 'the grace of
145 God', sir, and he hath 'enough'.

   Bassanio
Thou speak'st it well. Go, father, with thy son.
Take leave of thy old master, and inquire
My lodging out. [*To his* Servants] Give him a livery
More guarded than his fellows': see it done.

150   *in*: go inside—off the stage and, by implication, into Bassanio's house.

150-1   *I cannot . . . head*: Launcelot is joking by saying—here and in the rest of the speech—the opposite of what he means.

152   *table*: palm of the hand; Launcelot pretends to be a palmist, telling his fortune by looking at his hand.
  offer: promise.

153   *to swear upon a book*: to swear a legal oath it is customary to lay one's right hand on the Bible.

154   *line of life*: on the palm of the hand, a line passes round the ball of the thumb, and in palmistry this is called the line of life. Unbroken lines joining the base of the thumb to this line of life are said to indicate the number of wives that a man will have.
  trifle: minor matter.

156   *maids*: virgins.
  simple coming-in: modest income (Launcelot thinks of the dowries his wives will bring him).

157   *'scape*: escape.

159   *if Fortune be a woman*: the personification of Fortune is female, to indicate the inconstancy of Fate.

160   *gear*: business.

161   *in the twinkling*: in the twinkling of an eye (the time it takes to wink).

163   *orderly*: in order.
  bestow'd: put away (presumably on the boat for Belmont).

164   *feast*: give a banquet for.

166   *endeavours*: efforts.

170   *have a suit to you*: have a favour to ask you.

173   *rude*: unmannerly.
174   *Parts*: qualities.
  become thee: suit you.
177   *Something too liberal*: rather too freely.
  pain: care.

Launcelot
150 Father, in. I cannot get a service, no! I have ne'er a tongue in my head. Well, [*Looking at his hand*] if any man in Italy have a fairer table which doth offer to swear upon a book, I shall have good fortune. Go to; here's a simple line of life: here's a small trifle of
155 wives: alas! fifteen wives is nothing: eleven widows and nine maids is a simple coming-in for one man; and then to 'scape drowning thrice, and to be in peril of my life with the edge of a feather-bed; here are simple 'scapes. Well, if Fortune be a woman,
160 she's a good wench for this gear. Father, come; I'll take my leave of the Jew in the twinkling.
    [*Exeunt* Launcelot *and* Old Gobbo
Bassanio
I pray thee, good Leonardo, think on this.
These things being bought, and orderly bestow'd,
Return in haste, for I do feast tonight
165 My best-esteem'd acquaintance. Hie thee, go.
Leonardo
My best endeavours shall be done herein.

    Enter Gratiano
Gratiano
Where's your master?
Leonardo   Yonder, sir, he walks.
    [*Exit*
Gratiano
Signior Bassanio!
Bassanio
Gratiano!
Gratiano
170 I have a suit to you.
Bassanio   You have obtain'd it.
Gratiano
You must not deny me: I must go with you to Belmont.
Bassanio
Why, then you must. But hear thee, Gratiano;
Thou art too wild, too rude, and bold of voice—
Parts that become thee happily enough,
175 And in such eyes as ours appear not faults—
But where thou art not known, why, there they show
Something too liberal. Pray thee, take pain

178 To damp down with a drop of decency.
179 *skipping*: boisterous.
180 *misconster'd*: misunderstood.

182 *a sober habit*: both 'respectable clothes' and 'a serious manner'.
183 *but*: only.
185 *saying*: being said.
     hood: cover (hats were worn at meals in polite society).
187 *observance*: outward forms.
     civility: good manners.
188 *studied*: practised.
     sad: serious.
     ostent: appearance.
189 *grandam*: grandmother.
190 *bearing*: conduct.
191 *bar*: make an exception of.
     gauge: judge.
192 *were pity*: would be a pity.

194 *suit of mirth*: both 'amusing manner' and 'party dress'.
195 *purpose*: intend.

Act 2   Scene 3
Launcelot says goodbye to Shylock's daughter, Jessica, who is sorry to see him go.

3   *taste*: part.

To allay with some cold drops of modesty
Thy skipping spirit, lest, through thy wild behaviour,
180 I be misconster'd in the place I go to,
And lose my hopes.
     Gratiano   Signior Bassanio, hear me:
If I do not put on a sober habit,
Talk with respect, and swear but now and then,
Wear prayer-books in my pocket, look demurely,
185 Nay more, while grace is saying, hood mine eyes
Thus with my hat, and sigh, and say 'amen',
Use all the observance of civility,
Like one well studied in a sad ostent
To please his grandam, never trust me more.
     Bassanio
190 Well, we shall see your bearing.
     Gratiano
Nay, but I bar tonight; you shall not gauge me
By what we do tonight.
     Bassanio   No, that were pity:
I would entreat you rather to put on
Your boldest suit of mirth, for we have friends
195 That purpose merriment. But fare you well:
I have some business.
     Gratiano
And I must to Lorenzo and the rest;
But we will visit you at supper-time.   [*Exeunt*

Scene 3 *Venice. The street outside Shylock's house*

Enter Jessica *and* Launcelot
     Jessica
I am sorry thou wilt leave my father so:
Our house is hell, and thou, a merry devil,
Didst rob it of some taste of tediousness.
But fare thee well; there is a ducat for thee—
5 And, Launcelot, soon at supper shalt thou see
Lorenzo, who is thy new master's guest:
Give him this letter—do it secretly.
And so farewell: I would not have my father
See me in talk with thee.

Launcelot

10 Adieu! tears exhibit my tongue. Most beautiful
pagan, most sweet Jew! If a Christian do not play
the knave and get thee, I am much deceived. But,
adieu! these foolish drops do something drown my
manly spirit: adieu!

Jessica

15 Farewell, good Launcelot.   [*Exit* Launcelot
Alack, what heinous sin is it in me
To be asham'd to be my father's child!
But though I am a daughter to his blood,
I am not to his manners. O Lorenzo,
20 If thou keep promise, I shall end this strife,
Become a Christian, and thy loving wife.   [*Exit*

Scene 4 *Venice. The street outside Shylock's house*

     Enter Gratiano, Lorenzo, Salerio, *and*
     Solanio

Lorenzo

Nay, we will slink away in supper-time,
Disguise us at my lodging, and return
All in an hour.

Gratiano

We have not made good preparation.

Salerio

5 We have not spoke us yet of torch-bearers.

Solanio

'Tis vile unless it may be quaintly order'd,
And better, in my mind, not undertook.

Lorenzo

'Tis now but four o'clock: we have two hours
To furnish us.

     Enter Launcelot, *with a letter*
       Friend Launcelot, what's the news?

Launcelot

10 And it shall please you to break up this, it shall
seem to signify.

Lorenzo

I know the hand: in faith, 'tis a fair hand;
And whiter than the paper it writ on
Is the fair hand that writ.

---

10   *Adieu*: goodbye (French).
    exhibit: Launcelot means 'inhibit
my tongue' (= prevent me from
speaking).
13   *something*: somewhat, rather.

16   *heinous*: hateful.

19   *not to his manners*: not like him
in behaviour.
20   *keep promise*: keep your promise.

Act 2   Scene 4
Bassanio's friends have planned some
kind of entertainment to amuse the
guests at dinner. Launcelot gives
Lorenzo the letter from Jessica, and
Lorenzo explains his intentions to the
audience.

5   *spoke us*: ordered.

6   *quaintly order'd*: done with style.

9   *To furnish us*: to get ourselves
ready.

10   *And*: if.
    break up this: break the seal on
the letter.
11   *seem to signify*: inform you.
12   *know the hand*: recognize the
handwriting—but then Lorenzo goes
on to talk about 'the hand that writ'
(wrote) the letter.

Gratiano   Love news, in faith.
Launcelot

15   By your leave, sir.
Lorenzo
Whither goest thou?
Launcelot
Marry, sir, to bid my old master, the Jew, to sup
tonight with my new master, the Christian.
Lorenzo
Hold here, take this: tell gentle Jessica
20   I will not fail her; speak it privately.
Go, gentlemen,   [*Exit* Launcelot
Will you prepare you for this masque tonight?
I am provided of a torch-bearer.
Salerio
Ay, marry, I'll be gone about it straight.
Solanio
25   And so will I.
Lorenzo   Meet me and Gratiano
At Gratiano's lodging some hour hence.
Salerio
'Tis good we do so.
                    [*Exeunt* Salerio *and* Solanio
Gratiano
Was not that letter from fair Jessica?
Lorenzo
I must needs tell thee all. She hath directed
30   How I shall take her from her father's house;
What gold and jewels she is furnish'd with;
What page's suit she hath in readiness.
If e'er the Jew her father come to heaven,
It will be for his gentle daughter's sake;
35   And never dare misfortune cross her foot,
Unless she do it under this excuse,
That she is issue to a faithless Jew.
Come, go with me: peruse this as thou goest.
Fair Jessica shall be my torch-bearer.   [*Exeunt*

---

15   *By your leave*: with your per-
      mission (Launcelot asks if he may go).

17   *sup*: dine.

23   *provided of*: supplied with.

24   *straight*: immediately.

29   *I must needs tell thee all*: I've just
      got to tell you everything.
      directed: instructed.
31   *furnish'd* supplied.

34   *gentle*: Launcelot makes a pun
      with 'gentile' (a non-Jewish person).
35   *foot*: path.
36   *she*: i.e. misfortune (personified
      as female),
      under: with.
37   *she is . . . Jew*: Jessica is the
      offspring of a Jew who does not believe
      in the Christian faith.
38   *peruse*: study.

Act 2   Scene 5
Shylock instructs Jessica to lock up the house carefully; he then goes off to have dinner with Bassanio.

2   *of*: between.
3   *gormandize*: over-eat.

5   *rend apparel out*: wear holes in your clothes.

8   *wont*: accustomed.

11   *bid forth*: invited out.
12   *wherefore*: why.

15   *prodigal*: wasteful; see note to *I*, *I*, 129.
16   *Look to*: take care of.
      right loath: very reluctant.
17   There is some evil being plotted against my peace of mind.

20   *reproach*: Launcelot means 'approach'.
21   *So do I his*: i.e. his reproach; Shylock takes Launcelot's word, not his meaning.

23-7 *it was . . . afternoon*: Launcelot's nonsense, making fun of prophesying by omens: *Black Monday* is Easter Monday, and *Ash Wednesday* the first day of Lent.

Scene 5 *Venice. The street outside Shylock's house*

Enter Shylock *and* Launcelot

Shylock
Well, thou shalt see, thy eyes shall be thy judge
The difference of old Shylock and Bassanio—
What, Jessica!—thou shalt not gormandize
As thou hast done with me—What, Jessica!—
5 And sleep and snore, and rend apparel out—
Why, Jessica, I say!

Launcelot   Why, Jessica!

Shylock
Who bids thee call? I do not bid thee call.

Launcelot
Your worship was wont to tell me that I could do
nothing without bidding.

Enter Jessica

Jessica
10 Call you? What is your will?

Shylock
I am bid forth to supper, Jessica;
There are my keys. But wherefore should I go?
I am not bid for love: they flatter me.
But yet I'll go in hate, to feed upon
15 The prodigal Christian. Jessica, my girl,
Look to my house. I am right loath to go:
There is some ill a-brewing towards my rest,
For I did dream of money-bags tonight.

Launcelot
I beseech you, sir, go: my young master doth expect
20 your reproach.

Shylock
So do I his.

Launcelot
And they have conspired together: I will not say
you shall see a masque; but if you do, then it was
not for nothing that my nose fell a-bleeding on
25 Black Monday last, at six o'clock i' the morning,
falling out that year on Ash Wednesday was four
year in th' afternoon.

Shylock
What, are there masques? Hear you me, Jessica:
Lock up my doors, and when you hear the drum
30 And the vile squealing of the wry-neck'd fife,
Clamber not you up to the casements then,
Nor thrust your head into the public street
To gaze on Christian fools with varnish'd faces,
But stop my house's ears—I mean my casements—
35 Let not the sound of shallow foppery enter
My sober house. By Jacob's staff I swear
I have no mind of feasting forth tonight;
But I will go. Go you before me, sirrah;
Say I will come.
    Launcelot
40 I will go before, sir. Mistress, look out at window,
for all this:

    There will come a Christian by,
    Will be worth a Jewess' eye.
                                    [*Exit* Launcelot
    Shylock
What says that fool of Hagar's offspring, ha?
    Jessica
45 His words were, 'Farewell, mistress'; nothing else.
    Shylock
The patch is kind enough, but a huge feeder;
Snail-slow in profit, and he sleeps by day
More than the wild cat: drones hive not with me;
Therefore I part with him, and part with him
50 To one that I would have him help to waste
His borrow'd purse. Well, Jessica, go in—
Perhaps I will return immediately—
Do as I bid you; shut doors after you:
'Fast bind, fast find',
55 A proverb never stale in thrifty mind.   [*Exit*
    Jessica
Farewell; and if my fortune be not cross'd,
I have a father, you a daughter, lost.   [*Exit*

30   *wry-neck'd fife*: a fife is a small pipe which is played sideways, giving the player a twisted ('wry') neck.
31   *casements*: windows.
33   *varnish'd*: painted, or wearing masks.
35   *shallow foppery*: frivolity.
36   *Jacob's staff*: in Genesis 32: 10 Jacob boasts that he had only his staff when he crossed the river Jordan, yet he returned with two companies of men.
37   *forth*: away from home.

43   'Worth a Jew's eye' was a proverbial expression to indicate great value.
44   *Hagar*: the maid to Abraham's wife. Abraham was the father of her son, but he rejected the boy and sent him with his mother into the wilderness (Genesis, chapter 21).
46   *patch*: fool.
      huge feeder: he eats a lot.
47   *Snail-slow*: as slow as a snail.
      profit: learning his job.
48   *drones*: bees who do no work.
      hive: live (as in a bee-hive).
50   *waste*: ruin.

54   He who takes care of what he has will prosper.

56   *cross'd*: thwarted.

Act 2 Scene 6
Lorenzo and his friends meet outside
Shylock's house. Jessica appears on the
balcony, rather embarrassed because
she is dressed as a boy.

1   *penthouse*: porch.
2   *make stand*: wait.

4   Lovers always come before their
appointed hour.
5-7   Lovers are always in a greater
hurry to keep a new engagement than
they are to keep their marriage vows
('obliged faith') unbroken ('unforfeited').
5   *Venus' pigeons*: the classical
goddess of love rode in a chariot drawn
by doves.
8   *That ever holds*: that is always
true.
10   *untread*: retrace.
11   *tedious measures*: boring steps in
a formal riding exercise (which we now
call 'dressage').
    unbated: undiminished.
12   *pace*: perform.
14   *younger*: younger son, such as the
Prodigal Son in the parable (see note
to *1, 1*, 129).
15   *scarfed bark*: ship decorated with
flags and pennants.
16   *strumpet wind*: the wind is like
an unfaithful woman because it changes
so easily; the metaphor continues the
'Prodigal Son' allusion, because the son
wasted his money on prostitutes.
18   *over-weather'd ribs*: weather-
beaten sides.
19   *rent*: torn.
21   *abode*: delay.

Scene 6 *Venice. The street outside Shylock's house*

Enter Gratiano *and* Salerio *dressed as masquers*

Gratiano
This is the penthouse under which Lorenzo
Desir'd us to make stand.
Salerio   His hour is almost past.
Gratiano
And it is marvel he out-dwells his hour,
For lovers ever run before the clock.
Salerio
5 O ten times faster Venus' pigeons fly
To seal love's bonds new-made, than they are wont
To keep obliged faith unforfeited!
Gratiano
That ever holds: who riseth from a feast
With that keen appetite that he sits down?
10 Where is the horse that doth untread again
His tedious measures with the unbated fire
That he did pace them first? All things that are,
Are with more spirit chased than enjoy'd.
How like a younger or a prodigal
15 The scarfed bark puts from her native bay,
Hugg'd and embraced by the strumpet wind!
How like the prodigal doth she return,
With over-weather'd ribs and ragged sails,
Lean, rent, and beggar'd by the strumpet wind!

Enter Lorenzo

Salerio
20 Here comes Lorenzo: more of this hereafter.
Lorenzo
Sweet friends, your patience for my long abode;
Not I but my affairs have made you wait:
When you shall please to play the thieves for wives,
I'll watch as long for you then. Approach;
25 Here dwells my father Jew. Ho! who's within?

27   *tongue*: voice.

35   *exchange*: i.e. of clothes.

Enter Jessica *on the balcony, dressed as a boy*

Jessica
Who are you? Tell me, for more certainty,
Albeit I'll swear that I do know your tongue.

Lorenzo
Lorenzo, and thy love.

Jessica
Lorenzo, certain; and my love indeed,
30 For who love I so much? And now who knows
But you, Lorenzo, whether I am yours?

Lorenzo
Heaven and thy thoughts are witness that thou art.

Jessica
Here, catch this casket; it is worth the pains.
I am glad 'tis night, you do not look on me,
35 For I am much asham'd of my exchange:
But love is blind, and lovers cannot see
The pretty follies that themselves commit;
For if they could, Cupid himself would blush
To see me thus transformed to a boy.

Lorenzo

40 Descend, for you must be my torch-bearer.

Jessica

What! must I hold a candle to my shames?
They in themselves, good sooth, are too too light.
Why, 'tis an office of discovery, love,
And I should be obscur'd.

Lorenzo   So are you, sweet,

45 Even in the lovely garnish of a boy,
But come at once;
For the close night doth play the runaway,
And we are stay'd for at Bassanio's feast.

Jessica

I will make fast the doors, and gild myself

50 With some more ducats, and be with you straight.

[*Exit above*

Gratiano

Now, by my hood, a gentle, and no Jew.

Lorenzo

Beshrew me, but I love her heartily;
For she is wise, if I can judge of her;
And fair she is, if that mine eyes be true;

55 And true she is, as she hath prov'd herself;
And therefore, like herself, wise, fair, and true,
Shall she be placed in my constant soul.

Enter Jessica

What, art thou come? On, gentlemen; away!
Our masquing mates by this time for us stay.

[*Exeunt, except* Gratiano

Enter Antonio

Antonio

60 Who's there?

Gratiano

Signior Antonio!

Antonio

Fie, fie, Gratiano! where are all the rest?
'Tis nine o'clock; our friends all stay for you.
No masque tonight: the wind is come about;

65 Bassanio presently will go aboard:
I have sent twenty out to seek for you.

Gratiano

I am glad on't: I desire no more delight
Than to be under sail and gone tonight.   [*Exeunt*

---

42   *good sooth*: indeed.
     light: both 'obvious' and 'wanton'.
43   *an office of discovery*: a torch-bearer's job is to light up and reveal things.
44   *obscur'd*: concealed.
45   *garnish*: costume.
47   *close night*: night that hides our secret.
     doth play the runaway: is slipping away.
48   *stay'd*: waited.
49   *make fast*: lock.
     gild: adorn with gold.
50   *straight*: at once.
51   *by my hood*: upon my word.
     gentle: both 'gentle lady' and 'gentile'.
52   *Beshrew me*: curse me (a very mild oath, added only to intensify the declaration of love).
     heartily: with all my heart.
54   *be true*: see truly.
57   She shall always have a place in my soul.

63   *stay*: wait.
64   *is come about*: has changed direction.
65   *presently*: now.
     aboard: on to his ship.

68   *to be under sail*: to sail.

Act 2   Scene 7

The Prince of Morocco has come to examine the caskets. He reads aloud the inscription on each one, and tries to puzzle out the meanings. At last he makes his choice.

1   *discover*: reveal.

2   *several*: different.

8   *as blunt*: as dull as the lead.

9   *hazard*: risk.

12   *withal*: with the casket.

14   *back again*: in reverse order.

Scene 7 *Belmont. A room in Portia's house*

> *Enter* Portia, *with the* Prince of Morocco, *and their* Servants

Portia

Go, draw aside the curtains, and discover
The several caskets to this noble prince.

                [*The curtains are drawn back*

Now make your choice.

Morocco

The first, of gold, who this inscription bears:

5   '*Who chooseth me shall gain what many men desire*'.
The second, silver, which this promise carries:
'*Who chooseth me shall get as much as he deserves*'.
This third, dull lead, with warning all as blunt:
'*Who chooseth me must give and hazard all he hath*'.

10 How shall I know if I do choose the right?

Portia

The one of them contains my picture, prince:
If you choose that, then I am yours withal.

Morocco

Some god direct my judgment! Let me see:
I will survey th' inscriptions back again:

15 What says this leaden casket?
'*Who chooseth me must give and hazard all he hath.*'

19   *fair advantages*: good returns.
20   *dross*: rubbish (impure metal).
21   *nor . . . nor*: neither . . . nor.
22   *virgin hue*: colour of purity (white).

25   *even*: steady.
26   *rated*: assessed.
      thy estimation: your own estimation.
29-30 *to be . . . myself*: to be unsure of what I deserve is a sign of weakness, bringing discredit on ('disabling') myself.

36   *grav'd*: engraved.
      in gold: on the gold casket.

40   *mortal*: living.
41   *Hyrcanian deserts*: a savage region to the south of the Caspian Sea.
      vasty wilds: immense wildernesses.
42   *throughfares*: main roads.
44   *The watery kingdom*: the ocean.
44-5 *whose . . . heaven*: whose waves surge up as though they wanted to touch the sky, throwing spray (spitting) into the clouds.
45   *bar*: obstacle.
46   *foreign spirits*: suitors from abroad.
49   *Is 't like*: is it likely?
50-1 *it were . . . cerecloth*: lead would be too crude to enfold ('rib') the winding-sheet when she is buried.
52   *immur'd*: walled in.
53   *undervalu'd to*: less value than.
      tried: tested (without impurities).
54-5 Jewels as precious as Portia are never set in worse metal than gold.

Must give! For what? for lead? hazard for lead?
This casket threatens. Men that hazard all
Do it in hope of fair advantages:
20 A golden mind stoops not to shows of dross;
I'll then nor give nor hazard aught for lead.
What says the silver with her virgin hue?
'*Who chooseth me shall get as much as he deserves*'.
As much as he deserves! Pause there, Morocco,
25 And weigh thy value with an even hand.
If thou be'st rated by thy estimation,
Thou dost deserve enough; and yet enough
May not extend so far as to the lady:
And yet to be afeard of my deserving
30 Were but a weak disabling of myself.
As much as I deserve! Why, that's the lady:
I do in birth deserve her, and in fortunes,
In graces, and in qualities of breeding;
But more than these, in love I do deserve.
35 What if I stray'd no further, but chose here?
Let's see once more this saying grav'd in gold:
'*Who chooseth me shall gain what many men desire*'.
Why, that's the lady: all the world desires her;
From the four corners of the earth they come,
40 To kiss this shrine, this mortal breathing saint:
The Hyrcanian deserts and the vasty wilds
Of wide Arabia are as throughfares now
For princes to come view fair Portia:
The watery kingdom, whose ambitious head
45 Spits in the face of heaven, is no bar
To stop the foreign spirits, but they come,
As o'er a brook, to see fair Portia.
One of these three contains her heavenly picture.
Is 't like that lead contains her? 'Twere damnation
50 To think so base a thought: it were too gross
To rib her cerecloth in the obscure grave.
Or shall I think in silver she's immur'd,
Being ten times undervalu'd to tried gold?
O sinful thought! Never so rich a gem
55 Was set in worse than gold. They have in England

56   *A coin . . . angel*: the gold coin was in fact known as an 'angel'.

57   *insculp'd upon*: engraved on the surface of the coin.

61   *form*: picture.

63   *A carrion Death*: a skull.

65   *glisters*: glitters.
67   *his life hath sold*: has given his whole life.
68   *my outside*: the gilded outside of the casket.
69   *worms*: that feed on the bodies inside the 'Gilded tombs'.
71   *old*: experienced.
72   You would not have been given the answer written on this scroll.
73   *your suit is cold*: your hopes are dead.
77   *tedious*: lengthy, formal.
     part: depart.
78   *A gentle riddance*: a happy deliverance.
79   *complexion*: both 'colour' and 'personality'.

Act 2   Scene 8
Salerio and Solanio discuss a mystery—where is Lorenzo? Shylock (they have heard) has lost his daughter and been robbed of some money. There is bad news for Antonio.

1   *under sail*: set sail.
4   *raised*: roused from sleep (it was nine o'clock in scene 6, line 63).

A coin that bears the figure of an angel
Stamp'd in gold, but that's insculp'd upon;
But here an angel in a golden bed
Lies all within. Deliver me the key:
60 Here do I choose, and thrive I as I may!
      Portia
There, take it, prince; and if my form lie there,
Then I am yours.
                              [*He unlocks the golden casket*
      Morocco   O hell! what have we here?
A carrion Death, within whose empty eye
There is a written scroll. I'll read the writing.
65   *All that glisters is not gold;*
          Often have you heard that told:
          Many a man his life hath sold
          But my outside to behold:
          Gilded tombs do worms infold.
70   *Had you been as wise as bold,*
          Young in limbs, in judgment old,
          Your answer had not been inscroll'd.
          Fare you well, your suit is cold.

    Cold, indeed; and labour lost:
75   Then farewell heat, and welcome, frost!
Portia, adieu. I have too griev'd a heart
To take a tedious leave: thus losers part.
                              [*Exit with his* Servants
      Portia
A gentle riddance. Draw the curtains: go.
Let all of his complexion choose me so.   [*Exeunt*

Scene 8 *Venice. A street*

      Enter Salerio *and* Solanio
      Salerio
Why, man, I saw Bassanio under sail,
With him is Gratiano gone along;
And in their ship I am sure Lorenzo is not.
      Solanio
The villain Jew with outcries rais'd the duke,
5 Who went with him to search Bassanio's ship.

7   *given to understand*: told.
8   *gondola*: a flat-bottomed boat used on the canals of Venice.

10   *certified*: assured.

13   *variable*: because Shylock was crying for his daughter, his ducats, and revenge.

19   *double ducats*: worth double the value of ducats.

25   *look he keep his day*: be careful to pay his debt on the appointed day.
27   *reason'd*: talked.
28   *the narrow seas*: the English Channel.
     part: separate.
29   *miscarried*: perished.
30   *vessel*: ship.
     fraught: laden.

Salerio
He came too late, the ship was under sail,
But there the duke was given to understand
That in a gondola were seen together
Lorenzo and his amorous Jessica.
10 Besides, Antonio certified the duke
They were not with Bassanio in his ship.
Solanio
I never heard a passion so confus'd,
So strange, outrageous, and so variable,
As the dog Jew did utter in the streets:
15 'My daughter! O my ducats! O my daughter!
Fled with a Christian! O my Christian ducats!
Justice! the law! my ducats, and my daughter!
A sealed bag, two sealed bags of ducats,
Of double ducats, stol'n from me by my daughter!
20 And jewels! two stones, two rich and precious stones,
Stol'n by my daughter! Justice! find the girl!
She hath the stones upon her, and the ducats.'
Salerio
Why, all the boys in Venice follow him,
Crying his stones, his daughter, and his ducats.
Solanio
25 Let good Antonio look he keep his day,
Or he shall pay for this.
Salerio   Marry, well remember'd.
I reason'd with a Frenchman yesterday,
Who told me, in the narrow seas that part
The French and English, there miscarried
30 A vessel of our country richly fraught.

I thought upon Antonio when he told me,
And wish'd in silence that it were not his.
Solanio
You were best to tell Antonio what you hear;
Yet do not suddenly, for it may grieve him.
Salerio
35 A kinder gentleman treads not the earth.
I saw Bassanio and Antonio part:
Bassanio told him he would make some speed
Of his return: he answer'd, 'Do not so;
Slubber not business for my sake, Bassanio,
40 But stay the very riping of the time;
And for the Jew's bond which he hath of me,
Let it not enter in your mind of love:
Be merry, and employ your chiefest thoughts
To courtship and such fair ostents of love
45 As shall conveniently become you there.'
And even there, his eye being big with tears,
Turning his face, he put his hand behind him,
And with affection wondrous sensible
He wrung Bassanio's hand; and so they parted.
Solanio
50 I think he only loves the world for him.
I pray thee, let us go and find him out,
And quicken his embraced heaviness
With some delight or other.
Salerio   Do we so.
                                         [*Exeunt*

Scene 9 *Belmont. A room in Portia's house*

Enter Nerissa, *with a* Servant
Nerissa
Quick, quick, I pray thee; draw the curtain straight:
The Prince of Arragon hath ta'en his oath,
And comes to his election presently.
                    [*Curtains drawn to reveal caskets*

Enter the Prince of Arragon, Portia, *and*
Servants
Portia
Behold, there stand the caskets, noble prince:
5 If you choose that wherein I am contain'd,
Straight shall our nuptial rites be solemniz'd;

---

39   *Slubber not business*: do not hurry your business carelessly.
40   *the . . . time*: until the time is ripe, until the right moment.
41   *for*: as for.
42   Don't let it enter your head, which should be full of love.
44   *ostents*: demonstrations.
45   As shall be suitable and do you credit there.
46   *even there*: then and there.
47   *Turning*: turning away.
48   *wondrous sensible*: wonderfully tender.
50   I think he loves nothing else in the world so much as Bassanio.
52   *quicken*: enliven.
       his embraced heaviness: the sadness that he is indulging in.

Act 2   Scene 9
Another suitor, the Prince of Arragon, is to make his choice of the caskets. He reads the inscriptions, and meditates on what he deserves, before he opens one of the caskets. Just as he has read the scroll, news is brought that Bassanio is coming to Belmont.
1   *straight*: at once.
3   *to his election*: to make his choice.
       presently: now.

6   *solemniz'd*: performed.

9   *enjoin'd*: bound.

         observe: promise.

10   *unfold*: disclose.

14   *do fail . . . of*: am unlucky in.

17   *hazard*: gamble.

18   *so have I address'd me*: I have prepared in this way (by making the promises).

24-5   *that . . . multitude*: that word 'many' may refer to the foolish masses.

25   *show*: appearance.

26   Never knowing more than the foolish ('fond') eye can see.

27   *pries not*: does not look more closely.

         th'interior: the heart of the matter.

27-8   *the martlet . . . wall*: the house-martin, a bird that builds its nest in the open air ('weather') on the outside wall of a building.

29   Just in the way of accidents.

31   *jump*: go along with.

32   *rank me*: join.

37   *cozen*: cheat.

37-8   *be . . . merit*: pretend to be noble when he cannot show that he is worthy.

39   To put on nobleness (like a cloak) which he is not entitled to.

40   *estates*: positions of rank (such as lordships and knighthoods).

         degrees: social positions in an established hierarchy (an earl, for example, is superior to a viscount, and a viscount is superior to a baron).

         offices: appointments.

41   *deriv'd corruptly*: obtained by foul means.

42   *the wearer*: the holder of the titles. The clothing metaphor arises from the fact that on ceremonious occasions the members of different ranks wore (and still wear) distinctive robes.

43   *cover*: keep their hats on.

         bare: bareheaded, as a mark of respect to superiors—those who 'cover'.

45-6   *How . . . honour*: how many of those who should really be poor peasants could be picked out from the true sons of the nobility.

But if you fail, without more speech, my lord,
You must be gone from hence immediately.

    Arragon
I am enjoin'd by oath to observe three things:
10 First, never to unfold to any one
Which casket 'twas I chose; next, if I fail
Of the right casket, never in my life
To woo a maid in way of marriage; lastly,
If I do fail in fortune of my choice,
15 Immediately to leave you and be gone.

    Portia
To these injunctions every one doth swear
That comes to hazard for my worthless self.

    Arragon
And so have I address'd me. Fortune now
To my heart's hope! Gold, silver, and base lead.
20 '*Who chooseth me must give and hazard all he hath.*'
You shall look fairer, ere I give or hazard.
What says the golden chest? ha! let me see:
'*Who chooseth me shall gain what many men desire*'.
What many men desire! that 'many' may be meant
25 By the fool multitude, that choose by show,
Not learning more than the fond eye doth teach,
Which pries not to th' interior, but, like the martlet,
Builds in the weather on the outward wall,
Even in the force and road of casualty.
30 I will not choose what many men desire,
Because I will not jump with common spirits
And rank me with the barbarous multitudes.
Why, then to thee, thou silver treasure-house;
Tell me once more what title thou dost bear:
35 '*Who chooseth me shall get as much as he deserves*'.
And well said too; for who shall go about
To cozen fortune, and be honourable
Without the stamp of merit? Let none presume
To wear an undeserved dignity.
40 O that estates, degrees, and offices
Were not deriv'd corruptly, and that clear honour
Were purchas'd by the merit of the wearer.
How many then should cover that stand bare!
How many be commanded that command!
45 How much low peasantry would then be glean'd

46-8   *how much . . . new varnish'd*: how
much that is truly noble could be
sorted out from the modern rubbish
and restored to its original splendour.
48   *but to*: I must return to.
50   *I will . . . desert*: I will claim to
be deserving.
52   *Too long a pause.* Arragon is
speechless.
53   *blinking*: with goggling eyes.

54   *schedule*: scroll.
55   *thou*: i.e. the picture of the idiot.
60   To commit an offence and to
pass judgement on the offence are quite
separate actions (Arragon has done
wrong—in choosing the wrong casket
—but he is unable to judge himself).
62   *The fire . . . this*: for purification,
silver is refined in a furnace seven
times.
63-4   Perfect judgement, that never
makes a mistake, must be as refined as
silver.
64   *amiss*: wrongly.
65   *shadows kiss*: embrace illusions,
believe in what is not real.
66   *a shadow's bliss*: the illusion of
happiness.
67   *iwis*: indeed.
68   *Silver'd o'er*: covered in silver
(so that their folly is hidden).
69   *Take . . . bed.* This seems to
contradict the condition that the
unlucky suitor should never marry.
70   You will always be a fool.
71   *sped*: finished.
72-3   The longer I stay here, the
bigger fool I shall appear.

From the true seed of honour! and how much
  honour
Pick'd from the chaff and ruin of the times
To be new varnish'd! Well, but to my choice:
'*Who chooseth me shall get as much as he deserves*'.
50 I will assume desert. Give me a key for this,
And instantly unlock my fortunes here.
                              [*He opens the silver casket*
    Portia
Too long a pause for that which you find there.
    Arragon
What's here? the portrait of a blinking idiot,
Presenting me a schedule! I will read it.
55 How much unlike art thou to Portia!
How much unlike my hopes and my deservings!
'*Who chooseth me shall have as much as he deserves*'.
Did I deserve no more than a fool's head?
Is that my prize? are my deserts no better?
    Portia
60 To offend, and judge, are distinct offices,
And of opposed natures.
    Arragon   What is here?
The fire seven times tried this:
Seven times tried that judgment is
That did never choose amiss.
65 *Some there be that shadows kiss:*
Such have but a shadow's bliss.
There be fools alive, iwis,
Silver'd o'er; and so was this.
Take what wife you will to bed,
70 *I will ever be your head.*
So be gone: you are sped.

Still more fool I shall appear
By the time I linger here:
With one fool's head I came to woo,
75 But I go away with two.
Sweet, adieu. I'll keep my oath,
Patiently to bear my wrath.
                        [*Exit* Arragon *with his* Servants

78   *sing'd*: burned.
79   *deliberate fools*: fools who try to give reasons for their actions.
80   Their reasoning ('wit') gives them enough intelligence ('wisdom') to make the wrong choice, and lose.
81   *ancient saying*: proverb.
      heresy: falsehood.
82   *wiving*: marrying.

84   *what . . . lord*: what does my lord want? Portia is joking with her servant.
85   *alighted*: dismounted from his horse.
86   *before*: in advance.
87   *signify*: announce.
88   *sensible*: substantial (not simply words of greeting, but gifts).
      regreets: greetings.
89   *To wit*: that is to say.
      commends: compliments.
      breath: words.
91   *likely*: hopeful.
92   *A day in April*: in England this is sometimes quite warm and sunny, with a few green leaves on the trees, and flowers in bud.
93   *costly*: rich.
      at hand: coming soon.
94   *fore-spurrer*: herald, one who spurs on his horse on advance of the main party.
95   *afeard*: afraid.
96   *anon*: presently.
      some kin to thee: one of your relations.
97   *high-day wit*: special invention, suitable for a holiday.
99   *Cupid*: the classical god of love
      post: messenger.
      mannerly: courteously.
100   *Bassanio*: may it be Bassanio.

Portia
Thus hath the candle sing'd the moth.
O these deliberate fools! when they do choose,
80 They have the wisdom by their wit to lose.
      Nerissa
The ancient saying is no heresy:
'Hanging and wiving goes by destiny.'
      Portia
Come, draw the curtain, Nerissa.

                    Enter a Servant
      Servant
Where is my lady?
      Portia   Here; what would my lord?
      Servant
85 Madam, there is alighted at your gate
A young Venetian, one that comes before
To signify th' approaching of his lord;
From whom he bringeth sensible regreets,
To wit, besides commends and courteous breath,
90 Gifts of rich value. Yet I have not seen
So likely an ambassador of love.
A day in April never came so sweet
To show how costly summer was at hand,
As this fore-spurrer comes before his lord.
      Portia
95 No more, I pray thee: I am half afeard
Thou wilt say anon he is some kin to thee,
Thou spend'st such high-day wit in praising him.
Come, come, Nerissa; for I long to see
Quick Cupid's post that comes so mannerly.
      Nerissa
100 Bassanio, lord Love, if thy will it be!   [*Exeunt*

Act 3

Act 3 Scene 1
Salerio has heard bad news about one
of Antonio's ships. Shylock threatens
Antonio, and when Shylock and Tubal
are left on the stage together he gloats
over Antonio's danger. Shylock's
pleasure over this matter is equal to the
pain he suffers in the loss of his
daughter.

2   *yet it lives there*: there is still
a rumour.
           unchecked: undenied.
3   *lading*: cargo.
           the narrow seas: the English
Channel.
4   *the Goodwins*: the Goodwin
Sands, in the very middle of the
Channel.
5   *flat*: sandbank.
6   *tall*: fine.
6–7   *my gossip Report*: old mother
Rumour.
8   *gossip*: old woman.
           that: that report.
9   *knapped*: chewed.
           ginger. In Elizabethan drama old
people are often said to eat ginger, but
no-one seems to know why; perhaps it
warmed their stomachs, or aided
digestion.
11   *without . . . prolixity*: without
using any long and boring phrases.
11–12 *crossing . . . talk*: departing from
the straight line of conversation.

Scene 1 *Venice. A street*

Enter Solanio *and* Salerio

Solanio
Now, what news on the Rialto?

Salerio
Why, yet it lives there unchecked that Antonio hath
a ship of rich lading wrecked on the narrow seas—
the Goodwins, I think they call the place, a very
5 dangerous flat, and fatal, where the carcasses of
many a tall ship lie buried, as they say, if my gossip
Report be an honest woman of her word.

Solanio
I would she were as lying a gossip in that as ever
knapped ginger, or made her neighbours believe
10 she wept for the death of a third husband. But it is
true—without any slips of prolixity or crossing the
plain highway of talk—that the good Antonio, the
honest Antonio—O, that I had a title good enough
to keep his name company!

Salerio
15 Come, the full stop.

Solanio
Ha! what say'st thou? Why, the end is, he hath lost
a ship.

Salerio
I would it might prove the end of his losses.

15   *the full stop*: both 'come to the point' (in punctuation), and (from the technical terms of horse management) 'bring your horse from full gallop to a standstill'.

19-20   *Let . . . prayer*: when they say 'amen' (= so be it) at the end of a prayer, some Christians make the sign of the cross. Solanio puns on this meaning of 'cross' and the meaning 'frustrate', which is what the devil would do to his hopes for Antonio.

19   *betimes*: immediately.

26   *withal*: with.

28   *fledge*: fledged, having grown feathers on its wings.
      complexion: nature.
29   *dam*: mother.

31   *the devil*: i.e. Shylock himself (Salerio refers back to line 20).

33   *Out . . . carrion*: you dirty old man. Solanio pretends to think that Shylock meant his own body, rebelling in lust against the control of reason.

37   *Rhenish*: expensive white German wine.

39   *no*: not.

40   *match*: bargain.

42   *so smug*: looking so pleased with himself.

43   *mart*: stock exchange, the Rialto.
      look to: take care of.
44   *wont*: accustomed.

Solanio
Let me say 'amen' betimes, lest the devil cross my
20 prayer, for here he comes in the likeness of a Jew.

            Enter Shylock
How now, Shylock! what news among the
merchants?
Shylock
You knew, none so well, none so well as you, of my
daughter's flight.
Salerio
25 That's certain: I, for my part, knew the tailor that
made the wings she flew withal.
Solanio
And Shylock, for his own part, knew the bird was
fledge; and then it is the complexion of them all to
leave the dam.
Shylock
30 She is damned for it.
Salerio
That's certain, if the devil may be her judge.
Shylock
My own flesh and blood to rebel!
Solanio
Out upon it, old carrion! rebels it at these years?
Shylock
I say my daughter is my flesh and my blood.
Salerio
35 There is more difference between thy flesh and hers
than between jet and ivory; more between your
bloods than there is between red wine and Rhenish.
But tell us, do you hear whether Antonio have had
any loss at sea or no?
Shylock
40 There I have another bad match: a bankrupt,
a prodigal, who dare scarce show his head on the
Rialto; a beggar, that was used to come so smug
upon the mart. Let him look to his bond! he was
wont to call me usurer. Let him look to his bond!

45 he was wont to lend money for a Christian courtesy.
Let him look to his bond!

Salerio

Why, I am sure, if he forfeit thou wilt not take his
flesh: what's that good for?

Shylock

To bait fish withal: if it will feed nothing else, it
50 will feed my revenge. He hath disgraced me, and
hindered half a million, laughed at my losses,
mocked at my gains, scorned my nation, thwarted
my bargains, cooled my friends, heated mine
enemies; and what's his reason? I am a Jew. Hath
55 not a Jew eyes? hath not a Jew hands, organs,
dimensions, senses, affections, passions? fed with
the same food, hurt with the same weapons, subject
to the same diseases, healed by the same means,
warmed and cooled by the same winter and
60 summer, as a Christian is? If you prick us, do we
not bleed? if you tickle us, do we not laugh? if you
poison us, do we not die? and if you wrong us,
shall we not revenge? If we are like you in the rest,
we will resemble you in that. If a Jew wrong a
65 Christian, what is his humility? Revenge! If a
Christian wrong a Jew, what should his sufferance
be by Christian example? Why, revenge! The
villainy you teach me I will execute, and it shall go
hard but I will better the instruction.

Enter a Servant

Servant

70 Gentlemen, my master Antonio is at his house,
and desires to speak with you both.

Salerio

We have been up and down to seek him.

Enter Tubal

Solanio

Here comes another of the tribe: a third cannot
be matched, unless the devil himself turn Jew.

[*Exeunt* Solanio, Salerio *and* Servant

49   *To bait fish*: to use as bait for
fishing.
50   *disgraced*: dishonoured.
51   *hindered . . . million*: prevented
me from making half a million (ducats)
profit.
53   *bargains*: business deals.
       cooled: diminished their
affections.
       heated: encouraged their hatred.
56   *dimensions*: parts of the body.

65   *what is his humility*: what does
the Christian (who ought to bear his
sufferings with humility) do?
66-7   *what . . . be*: how should he
endure it?
68-9   *it shall . . . instruction*: if you are
not very careful, I shall do even more
harm than you have taught me to do.

72   We have been looking everywhere for him.

73-4   *a third . . . matched*: there is not
another Jew to equal these two.

Shylock

75 How now, Tubal! what news from Genoa? Hast thou found my daughter?

Tubal

I often came where I did hear of her, but cannot find her.

Shylock

Why there, there, there, there! a diamond gone,
80 cost me two thousand ducats in Frankfurt! The curse never fell upon our nation till now; I never felt it till now: two thousand ducats in that, and other precious, precious jewels. I would my daughter were dead at my foot, and the jewels in
85 her ear! would she were hearsed at my foot, and the ducats in her coffin! No news of them—why so? and I know not what's spent in the search. Why thou—loss upon loss! the thief gone with so much, and so much to find the thief; and no satisfaction,
90 no revenge: nor no ill luck stirring but what lights o' my shoulders; no sighs but o' my breathing; no tears but o' my shedding.

Tubal

Yes, other men have ill luck too. Antonio, as I heard in Genoa—

Shylock

95 What, what, what? ill luck? ill luck?

Tubal

—hath an argosy cast away, coming from Tripolis.

Shylock

I thank God! I thank God! Is it true? is it true?

Tubal

I spoke with some of the sailors that escaped the wreck.

Shylock

100 I thank thee, good Tubal. Good news, good news! ha, ha! Heard in Genoa?

Tubal

Your daughter spent in Genoa, as I heard, one night, fourscore ducats.

80-1 *The curse . . . nation*: God cursed the Jews because they disobeyed His law, and condemned them to exile (Daniel 9:11).

85 *hearsed*: laid in her coffin.

90 *lights o'*: lands on.
91 *but o' my breathing*: except the sighs that I breathe.

96 *argosy*: merchant ship.
cast away: wrecked.

102-3 *one night*: on one night.

105   *at a sitting*: on a single occasion.

107   *divers*: several.
107-8 *in my company*: along with me.
109   *break*: go bankrupt.

112   *of*: from.

114   *Out upon her*: damn her.
115   *had it of Leah*: it was a present from Leah (his wife—now presumably dead).

119-20 *fee me an officer*: hire a sheriff's officer for me. This was the normal procedure for arresting a debtor—Shylock is *not* suggesting a bribe.
120   *bespeak . . . before*: order him to be ready two weeks before Antonio's debt is due to be repaid.
122   *merchandise*: business.
123   *synagogue*: the Jewish temple.

Shylock
Thou stick'st a dagger in me: I shall never see my
105 gold again: fourscore ducats at a sitting! fourscore ducats!

Tubal
There came divers of Antonio's creditors in my company to Venice, that swear he cannot choose but break.

Shylock
110 I am very glad of it: I'll plague him; I'll torture him: I am glad of it.

Tubal
One of them showed me a ring that he had of your daughter for a monkey.

Shylock
Out upon her! Thou torturest me, Tubal: it was
115 my turquoise; I had it of Leah when I was a bachelor: I would not have given it for a wilderness of monkeys.

Tubal
But Antonio is certainly undone.

Shylock
Nay, that's true, that's very true. Go, Tubal, fee
120 me an officer; bespeak him a fortnight before. I will have the heart of him, if he forfeit; for, were he out of Venice, I can make what merchandise I will. Go, Tubal, and meet me at our synagogue; go, good Tubal; at our synagogue, Tubal.

[*Exeunt in different directions*

Act 3   Scene 2

Portia has fallen in love with Bassanio and wants him to wait a few days before making his choice of the caskets. But Bassanio refuses to wait. He meditates aloud on the difference between appearance and reality, and then chooses the leaden casket and wins Portia for his wife. Nerissa and Gratiano congratulate him, and Gratiano declares his own marriage plans. Lorenzo and Jessica arrive at Belmont, together with Salerio, who has brought a letter from Antonio. Antonio has written to say that he is in Shylock's power.

1   *tarry*: wait.
2   *hazard*: take this risk.
5   *I would not*: I don't want to.
6   Hatred does not give this kind of advice.
8   Portia seems to be saying that her speech should be easily understood because it is a simple expression of her thoughts (without the obscurities created by elaborate language).
10   *venture for me*: try to win me.
11   *I am forsworn*: I would have broken my promise.
12   *miss*: lose.
13-14   *wish . . . forsworn*: wish I had committed the sin of breaking my promise.
14   *Beshrew*: shame on.
15   *o'erlook'd*: bewitched.
18-19   *O these . . . rights*: in these wicked times there are obstacles to prevent owners from taking possession of the things they own.
20   *Prove it so*: if this proves to be the case (i.e. that Bassanio cannot possess her).
21   It will be fortune's fault, not mine.
22   *peise*: measure out.
23   *eke it*: add to it.
24   *To . . . election*: to hold you back from making your choice.
25   *the rack*: an instrument of torture which stretched the victim's body (as Portia is trying to stretch out the time) until he confessed his crimes—usually of treason to the state.

Scene 2 *Belmont. A room in Portia's house*

Enter Bassanio, Portia, Gratiano, Nerissa, *and* Servants

Portia
I pray you, tarry, pause a day or two
Before you hazard; for, in choosing wrong,
I lose your company: therefore, forbear awhile.
There's something tells me (but it is not love)
5   I would not lose you; and you know yourself,
Hate counsels not in such a quality.
But lest you should not understand me well—
And yet a maiden hath no tongue but thought—
I would detain you here some month or two
10   Before you venture for me. I could teach you
How to choose right, but then I am forsworn;
So will I never be: so may you miss me—
But if you do, you'll make me wish a sin,
That I had been forsworn. Beshrew your eyes,
15   They have o'erlook'd me and divided me:
One half of me is yours, the other half yours—
Mine own, I would say; but if mine, then yours,
And so all yours. O these naughty times
Put bars between the owners and their rights;
20   And so, though yours, not yours. Prove it so,
Let fortune go to hell for it, not I.
I speak too long; but 'tis to peise the time,
To eke it and to draw it out in length,
To stay you from election.
Bassanio   Let me choose;
25   For as I am, I live upon the rack.
Portia
Upon the rack, Bassanio! then confess
What treason there is mingled with your love.
Bassanio
None but that ugly treason of mistrust,
Which makes me fear th' enjoying of my love:
30   There may as well be amity and life
'Tween snow and fire, as treason and my love.
Portia
Ay, but I fear you speak upon the rack,
Where men enforced do speak anything.

29 *fear th' enjoying of my love*: afraid that I shall not have the one I love for my wife.

30 *amity*: friendship.

33 *enforced*: compelled (by torture).

35 *confess, and live*: this was offered to traitors on the rack, as the alternative to dying with their secrets.

36 Would be all that I have to confess.

38 *for deliverance*: to be released.

42 *aloof*: out of the way.

44 *a swan-like end*: the Elizabethans believed that the swan (which has no voice at all) sings only once, just before it dies.

45 *Fading*: dying.

46 *stand more proper*: fit more exactly.

46-7 *my eye . . . for him*: I shall weep, so he will seem to drown in my tears.

49 *flourish*: ceremonial fanfare on trumpets.

51 *dulcet*: sweet.
    in: at.

54 *presence*: handsome appearance.

55 *Alcides*: Hercules (son of Alcaeus). He rescued a Trojan princess, Hesione, who was being sacrificed (a 'virgin tribute') to a sea-monster. His motive was not love, however: he wanted her father's horses.

58 *aloof*: apart.
    Dardanian: Trojan (the descendants of Dardanus, who founded Troy).

59 *bleared visages*: tear-stained faces.

60 *issue*: outcome.

61 *Live thou*: if you live.
    dismay: alarm.

62 *fray*: fighting.

63 *fancy*: attraction.

64 *Or . . . or*: either . . . or.

67-9 Appearance is what first attracts one person to another, and the attraction grows stronger the more the couple look at each other. But fancy has a very short life.

Bassanio
Promise me life, and I'll confess the truth.
Portia
35 Well, then, confess, and live.
Bassanio   'Confess and love'
Had been the very sum of my confession:
O happy torment, when my torturer
Doth teach me answers for deliverance!
But let me to my fortune and the caskets.
Portia
40 Away then! I am lock'd in one of them:
If you do love me, you will find me out.
Nerissa and the rest, stand all aloof.
Let music sound while he doth make his choice;
Then, if he lose, he makes a swan-like end,
45 Fading in music: that the comparison
May stand more proper, my eye shall be the stream
And watery death-bed for him. He may win;
And what is music then? then music is
Even as the flourish when true subjects bow
50 To a new-crowned monarch: such it is
As are those dulcet sounds in break of day
That creep into the dreaming bridegroom's ear,
And summon him to marriage. Now he goes,
With no less presence, but with much more love,
55 Than young Alcides, when he did redeem
The virgin tribute paid by howling Troy
To the sea-monster: I stand for sacrifice;
The rest aloof are the Dardanian wives,
With bleared visages come forth to view
60 The issue of th' exploit. Go, Hercules!
Live thou, I live: with much, much more dismay
I view the fight than thou that mak'st the fray.
[*A Song, whilst* Bassanio *comments on the caskets to himself*

    Tell me where is fancy bred,
    Or in the heart or in the head?
65 *How begot, how nourished?*
      Reply, reply.
    It is engend'red in the eyes,
    With gazing fed; and fancy dies
    In the cradle where it lies.
70   *Let us all ring fancy's knell:*
    I'll begin it—Ding, dong, bell.
    Ding, dong, bell.

70   *knell*: funeral bell.
73   *least themselves*: not at all what they appear to be.
74   *The world*: people.
75-7   *In law . . . evil*: in legal matters, the most rotten case can be presented so well that the presentation conceals the evil (just as bad—'tainted'—meat can be spiced—'seasoned'—to hide the real taste).
78-9   *What . . . text*: a great sin ('damned error') can be committed by a man with a pious appearance ('sober brow') who is able to quote the Bible and excuse ('approve') what he is doing (see also *1, 3, 94*).
81   *There . . . simple*: both 'no vice is so plain' and 'no vicious man is so foolish'.
81-2   *but . . . parts*: that the vice (or the vicious man) does not have the outward appearance of virtue.
84   *stairs of sand*: sandbanks.
        yet: nevertheless.
85   *Hercules*: the superman of classical mythology.
        Mars: the classical god of war.
86   *inward search'd*: if their intestines are examined.
        livers . . . milk: a brave man's liver should (the Elizabethans thought) be red with blood (see note on *1, 1, 80*).
87   *valour's excrement*: the hairy growth ('beards') of courage.
88   *render them redoubted*: make them seem terrible.
        beauty: cosmetics.
89-91   Those who wear the heaviest make-up which has been bought by the ounce ('purchas'd by the weight') are the most immoral ('lightest'). The two senses of 'light' (in weight and in morals) allow Bassanio to point out the paradox, the 'miracle in nature'.
92-6   The golden curls on a woman's head may be no more than a wig, made from the hair of some other woman, now dead. The adjective 'snaky' implies a comparison with the head of Medusa, who had snakes for hair; anyone who looked at Medusa was turned to stone.

Bassanio

So may the outward shows be least themselves:
The world is still deceiv'd with ornament.
75 In law, what plea so tainted and corrupt
But, being season'd with a gracious voice,
Obscures the show of evil? In religion,
What damned error, but some sober brow
Will bless it and approve it with a text,
80 Hiding the grossness with fair ornament?
There is no vice so simple but assumes
Some mark of virtue on his outward parts.
How many cowards, whose hearts are all as false
As stairs of sand, wear yet upon their chins
85 The beards of Hercules and frowning Mars,
Who, inward search'd, have livers white as milk;
And these assume but valour's excrement
To render them redoubted. Look on beauty,
And you shall see 'tis purchas'd by the weight;
90 Which therein works a miracle in nature,
Making them lightest that wear most of it:
So are those crisped snaky golden locks
Which make such wanton gambols with the wind,
Upon supposed fairness, often known
95 To be the dowry of a second head,
The skull that bred them in the sepulchre.
Thus ornament is but the guiled shore
To a most dangerous sea, the beauteous scarf
Veiling an Indian beauty; in a word,
100 The seeming truth which cunning times put on
To entrap the wisest. Therefore, thou gaudy gold,
Hard food for Midas, I will none of thee;
Nor none of thee, thou pale and common drudge
'Tween man and man: but thou, thou meagre lead,
105 Which rather threaten'st than dost promise aught,
Thy paleness moves me more than eloquence,
And here choose I: joy be the consequence!

Portia

[*Aside*] How all the other passions fleet to air,
As doubtful thoughts, and rash-embrac'd despair,

92   *crisped*: curled.
95   *dowry of*: endowment (legacy)
from.
97   *guiled*: treacherous.
99   *Indian*: dark-skinned. The
Elizabethan ideal of beauty was
blonde, with a fair skin; 'an Indian
beauty' would be almost a contra-
diction in terms.
99   *in a word*: briefly.
102   *Midas*: in Greek mythology,
Midas was granted his wish that everything he touched should be turned to
gold; food became a problem for him.
will none of thee: will not have
anything to do with you.
104   *meagre*: unattractive.
105   Who makes threats rather than
promises (in the inscription on the
casket).
107   *consequence*: i.e. of the choice.
108   *fleet to*: vanish into.
109   *As*: such as.
rash-embrac'd: too quickly
accepted.
110   *green eyed*: green was the colour
associated with jealousy (in England we
still say 'green with envy').
111   *allay*: diminish.
112   *measure*: moderation.
scant: restrain.
115   *counterfeit*: image.
115-16 *What . . . creation*: the artist
must have been almost divine, because
he has made a picture which is so like
life.
Move these eyes: do the eyes
move.
117-18 Or is it rather that, because they
seem to be fixed ('riding') on my own
eyeballs, they appear to be moving.
118   *sever'd*: parted.
119-20 *so sweet . . . friends*: it is right
that such a sweet barrier (Portia's
breath) should separate such sweet
friends (her lips).
120-3   *Here . . . cobwebs*: in this picture,
the painter has been like a spider,
because the hair is like a golden net-
work ('mesh'), which traps men's
hearts just as gnats are caught in
spiders' webs.

110 And shuddering fear, and green-eyed jealousy.
O love be moderate, allay thy ecstasy,
In measure rain thy joy, scant this excess,
I feel too much thy blessing; make it less,
For fear I surfeit!
Bassanio   What find I here?
[He opens the leaden casket
115 Fair Portia's counterfeit! What demi-god
Hath come so near creation? Move these eyes?
Or whether, riding on the balls of mine,
Seem they in motion? Here are sever'd lips,
Parted with sugar breath; so sweet a bar
120 Should sunder such sweet friends. Here in her hairs
The painter plays the spider, and hath woven
A golden mesh t' entrap the hearts of men
Faster than gnats in cobwebs: but her eyes!
How could he see to do them? having made one,
125 Methinks it should have power to steal both his
And leave itself unfurnish'd: yet look how far
The substance of my praise doth wrong this shadow
In underprizing it, so far this shadow
Doth limp behind the substance. Here's the scroll,
130 The continent and summary of my fortune.

You that choose not by the view,
Chance as fair, and choose as true!
Since this fortune falls to you,
Be content and seek no new.
135 *If you be well pleas'd with this*
And hold your fortune for your bliss,
Turn you where your lady is
And claim her with a loving kiss.

A gentle scroll. Fair lady, by your leave;
[Kissing her
140 I come by note, to give and to receive.
Like one of two contending in a prize,

124-6   *having . . . unfurnis'd*: I think that when one eye had been painted, it would have the power (with its beauty) to blind the painter (stealing away his eyes) so that he could not paint the second eye.

126   *unfurnish'd*: not provided with a companion.

126-9   *yet look . . . substance*: I know that my praise is inadequate ('doth wrong') the portrait (which is only a sketch—'shadow' of Portia), and cannot speak its true worth (underprizes it). In the same way, the portrait ('shadow') is far behind the real thing.

130   *continent*: container.

131   *by the view*: from the outside appearance.

132   May you always have such good fortune ('Chance') and choose as well (as you have done this time).

136   And think ('hold') that your luck ('fortune') means happiness.

140   *by note*: as instructed.

143   *universal shout*: shouts of approval from everyone.

144   *Giddy in spirit*: dazed.

145   *his or no*: for him or not.

148   *ratified*: validated, given authority.

155   *That only*: only in order to.
         account: estimation.

156   *livings*: possessions.

157   *Exceed account*: be worth more than can be reckoned.

157-9   *but . . . unpractis'd*: the full amount of me is no more than the full amount of something that, at best ('to term in gross'), is a girl with no education, no training, no experience.

160   *Happy*: fortunate.

162   *is not bred so dull*: was not born so stupid.

166-7   *Myself . . . converted*: I now belong, with all that I possess, to you.

167   *but now*: just a moment ago.

174   *vantage*: opportunity.
         exclaim on: accuse.

175   *bereft me of*: stolen from me.

176   *my blood speaks*: Bassanio is blushing.

That thinks he hath done well in people's eyes,
Hearing applause and universal shout,
Giddy in spirit, still gazing in a doubt
145 Whether those peals of praise be his or no;
So, thrice-fair lady, stand I, even so,
As doubtful whether what I see be true,
Until confirm'd, sign'd, ratified by you.

Portia
You see me, Lord Bassanio, where I stand,
150 Such as I am: though for myself alone
I would not be ambitious in my wish,
To wish myself much better; yet, for you,
I would be trebled twenty times myself;
A thousand times more fair, ten thousand times more rich;
155 That only to stand high in your account,
I might in virtues, beauties, livings, friends,
Exceed account: but the full sum of me
Is sum of something, which, to term in gross,
Is an unlesson'd girl, unschool'd, unpractis'd;
160 Happy in this, she is not yet so old
But she may learn; happier than this,
She is not bred so dull but she can learn;
Happiest of all, is that her gentle spirit
Commits itself to yours to be directed
165 As from her lord, her governor, her king.
Myself and what is mine, to you and yours
Is now converted: but now I was the lord
Of this fair mansion, master of my servants,
Queen o'er myself; and even now, but now,
170 This house, these servants, and this same myself
Are yours, my lord's. I give them with this ring;
Which when you part from, lose, or give away,
Let it presage the ruin of your love,
And be my vantage to exclaim on you.

Bassanio
175 Madam, you have bereft me of all words,
Only my blood speaks to you in my veins;
And there is such confusion in my powers,
As, after some oration fairly spoke
By a beloved prince, there doth appear
180 Among the buzzing pleased multitude;

177-80   My thoughts are confused, just like a crowd of happy, murmuring citizens who have heard a fine speech from a much-loved ruler.

181-2   When everything is so mixed up that it becomes a wilderness where nothing can be distinguished except ('save of') joy.

187   *prosper*: be fulfilled.

190   I hope that you will have all the happiness that you can wish for yourselves.

191   You cannot wish for any more than I wish for you.

192   *solemnize*: celebrate formally.

193   *bargain of your faith*: contract of your love.

194   *Even at that time*: at that very same time

195   *so*: provided that.

199-200   *intermission . . . you*: time-wasting no more belongs to me than to you—I don't waste any more time than you do.

201   *stood*: depended.

202   *as the matter falls*: as it happens.

203   *until I sweat again*: so hard that I was sweating.

204   *swearing*: declaring my love.
    roof: i.e. the roof of his mouth.

205   *if promise last*: if she keeps her promise. Gratiano puns with two senses of a word, here and in line 211.

206   *of*: from.

209   *so*: if.
    stand: are.

211   *faith*: in good faith.

213-14   We'll bet them that whoever gets the first son wins a thousand ducats.

Where every something, being blent together,
Turns to a wild of nothing, save of joy,
Express'd, and not express'd. But when this ring
Parts from this finger, then parts life from hence:
185 O then be bold to say Bassanio's dead.

Nerissa
My lord and lady, it is now our time,
That have stood by and seen our wishes prosper,
To cry, good joy. Good joy, my lord and lady!

Gratiano
My Lord Bassanio, and my gentle lady,
190 I wish you all the joy that you can wish;
For I am sure you can wish none from me.
And when your honours mean to solemnize
The bargain of your faith, I do beseech you,
Even at that time I may be married too.

Bassanio
195 With all my heart, so thou canst get a wife.

Gratiano
I thank your lordship, you have got me one.
My eyes, my lord, can look as swift as yours:
You saw the mistress, I beheld the maid;
You lov'd, I lov'd: for intermission
200 No more pertains to me, my lord, than you.
Your fortune stood upon the caskets there,
And so did mine too, as the matter falls;
For wooing here until I sweat again,
And swearing till my very roof was dry
205 With oaths of love, at last (if promise last)
I got a promise of this fair one here
To have her love, provided that your fortune
Achiev'd her mistress.

Portia   Is this true, Nerissa?

Nerissa
Madam, it is, so you stand pleas'd withal.

Bassanio
210 And do you, Gratiano, mean good faith?

Gratiano
Yes, faith, my lord.

Bassanio
Our feast shall be much honour'd in your marriage.

Gratiano
We'll play with them the first boy for a thousand ducats.

215   *and stake down*: with our money
down on the table (to show that the
bet is serious). Gratiano replies with a
bawdy joke, pretending that Nerissa
means 'with weapon down'.

217   *infidel*: non-believer (a reference
to Jessica's Jewishness).

220-1   If I have the right ('power') to
welcome you here, since my claim
('interest') to this place is so new
(young).

222   *very*: true.

226   *My purpose was not*: I did not
intend.

227   *by the way*: by chance.

228   *past . . . nay*: and would not let
me refuse.

231   *Commends him*: sends his
greetings.

235   *estate*: condition.

236   *yond*: yonder.

238   *royal*: honourable.

240   *Jasons*: see note on *1, 1, 170*.

Nerissa
215   What, and stake down?
Gratiano
No, we shall ne'er win at that sport and stake down!
But who comes here? Lorenzo and his infidel!
What! and my old Venetian friend, Salerio?

Enter Lorenzo, Jessica, *and* Salerio
Bassanio
Lorenzo, and Salerio, welcome hither,
220   If that the youth of my new interest here
Have power to bid you welcome. By your leave,
I bid my very friends and countrymen,
Sweet Portia, welcome.
Portia   So do I, my lord:
They are entirely welcome.
Lorenzo
225   I thank your honour. For my part, my lord,
My purpose was not to have seen you here,
But meeting with Salerio by the way,
He did entreat me, past all saying nay,
To come with him along.
Salerio   I did, my lord,
230   And I have reason for it. Signior Antonio
Commends him to you.   [*Gives* Bassanio *a letter*
Bassanio   Ere I ope his letter,
I pray you, tell me how my good friend doth.
Salerio
Not sick, my lord, unless it be in mind;
Nor well, unless in mind: his letter there
235   Will show you his estate.
                              [Bassanio *opens the letter*
Gratiano
Nerissa, cheer yond stranger; bid her welcome.
Your hand, Salerio. What's the news from Venice?
How doth that royal merchant, good Antonio?
I know he will be glad of our success;
240   We are the Jasons, we have won the fleece.
Salerio
I would you had won the fleece that he hath lost.

242   *shrewd*: bitter.

245   *constitution*: complexion.
246   *constant*: normal.
247   *With leave*: excuse me.

251   *blotted paper*: spoiled a paper with ink.
253   *freely*: honestly.
254   *Ran in my veins*: was in my blood.
256   *Rating*: valuing.
257   *was a braggart*: boasted.
258   *state*: estate, fortune.

260   *engag'd*: bound.
261   *mere*: absolute.
262   *To feed my means*: to get the money I needed.
263   *as*: is like.
265   *Issuing life-blood*: from which his life-blood pours.
266   *ventures*: business speculations.
        hit: success.

270   *merchant-marring rocks*: rocks that ruin merchants.

272   *present*: ready.
        discharge: pay his debt to.

275   *confound*: ruin.
276   *plies*: urges his case on.
277   *impeach*: question.
        freedom of the state: the integrity of the law in Venice.
279   *magnificoes*: noblemen.
280   *port*: authority.

Portia
There are some shrewd contents in yond same paper,
That steals the colour from Bassanio's cheek:
Some dear friend dead, else nothing in the world
245 Could turn so much the constitution
Of any constant man. What, worse and worse!
With leave, Bassanio; I am half yourself,
And I must freely have the half of anything
That this same paper brings you.
Bassanio   O sweet Portia!
250 Here are a few of the unpleasant'st words
That ever blotted paper. Gentle lady,
When I did first impart my love to you,
I freely told you all the wealth I had
Ran in my veins—I was a gentleman—
255 And then I told you true; and yet, dear lady,
Rating myself at nothing, you shall see
How much I was a braggart. When I told you
My state was nothing, I should then have told you
That I was worse than nothing; for, indeed,
260 I have engag'd myself to a dear friend,
Engag'd my friend to his mere enemy,
To feed my means. Here is a letter, lady;
The paper as the body of my friend,
And every word in it a gaping wound,
265 Issuing life-blood. But is it true, Salerio?
Hath all his ventures fail'd? What, not one hit?
From Tripolis, from Mexico, and England,
From Lisbon, Barbary, and India?
And not one vessel 'scape the dreadful touch
270 Of merchant-marring rocks?
Salerio   Not one, my lord.
Besides, it should appear, that if he had
The present money to discharge the Jew,
He would not take it. Never did I know
A creature, that did bear the shape of man,
275 So keen and greedy to confound a man.
He plies the duke at morning and at night,
And doth impeach the freedom of the state,
If they deny him justice: twenty merchants,
The duke himself, and the magnificoes
280 Of greatest port, have all persuaded with him;

281   *drive him from*: persuade him to give up.
       envious plea: malicious claim.

284   *his countrymen*: fellow Jews.

288   *deny not*: do not prevent it.
289   *hard*: badly.

292-3   *The . . . courtesies*: a man whose spirit is the most willing and untiring in helping others.
294   *The ancient Roman honour*: i.e. loyalty to friends and country.

298   *deface*: cancel.

302   *call me wife*: make me your wife.

310   *shall hence*: must go away from here.
311   *cheer*: face.
312   *dear bought*: expensively purchased.

But none can drive him from the envious plea
Of forfeiture, of justice, and his bond.
Jessica
When I was with him, I have heard him swear
To Tubal and to Chus, his countrymen,
285 That he would rather have Antonio's flesh
Than twenty times the value of the sum
That he did owe him; and I know, my lord,
If law, authority, and power deny not,
It will go hard with poor Antonio.
Portia
290 Is it your dear friend that is thus in trouble?
Bassanio
The dearest friend to me, the kindest man,
The best-condition'd and unwearied spirit
In doing courtesies, and one in whom
The ancient Roman honour more appears
295 Than any that draws breath in Italy.
Portia
What sum owes he the Jew?
Bassanio
For me, three thousand ducats.
Portia   What, no more?
Pay him six thousand, and deface the bond;
Double six thousand, and then treble that,
300 Before a friend of this description
Shall lose a hair through Bassanio's fault.
First go with me to church and call me wife,
And then away to Venice to your friend;
For never shall you lie by Portia's side
305 With an unquiet soul. You shall have gold
To pay the petty debt twenty times over:
When it is paid, bring your true friend along.
My maid Nerissa and myself meantime
Will live as maids and widows. Come, away!
310 For you shall hence upon your wedding-day.
Bid your friends welcome, show a merry cheer;
Since you are dear bought, I will love you dear.
But let me hear the letter of your friend.

314   *miscarried*: been lost.

317   *cleared*: cancelled.
318   *but*: only.
319   *use your pleasure*: do as you
please.

321   *O love*: Portia speaks as though
Antonio's reference to Bassanio's 'love'
was meant for her.
      dispatch: hurry up with.
322   *good leave*: kind permission.
324–5   I shall not go to bed, and not
even rest shall come between us.
325   *twain*: two.

Act 3   Scene 3
Antonio has been arrested and taken to
prison. Shylock threatens him, but
Antonio is patient.

1   *look to him*: guard him carefully.
2   *gratis*: free of interest.

4   *speak not*: don't argue.

9   *naughty*: worthless.
    fond: foolish.
10 *abroad*: out of the prison.

14 *dull-eyed*: stupid.

16 *intercessors*: pleaders.

Bassanio
Sweet Bassanio, my ships have all miscarried, my
315 *creditors grow cruel, my estate is very low, my bond to*
the Jew is forfeit; and since, in paying it, it is impossible
I should live, all debts are cleared between you and
I, if I might but see you at my death. Notwithstanding,
use your pleasure: if your love do not persuade you
320 *to come, let not my letter.*
Portia
O love, dispatch all business, and be gone!
Bassanio
Since I have your good leave to go away,
I will make haste; but, till I come again,
No bed shall e'er be guilty of my stay,
325 Nor rest be interposer 'twixt us twain.   [*Exeunt*

Scene 3 *Venice. A street*

Enter Shylock, Solanio, Antonio, *and*
Gaoler
Shylock
Gaoler, look to him: tell not me of mercy;
This is the fool that lent out money gratis:
Gaoler, look to him.
Antonio   Hear me yet, good Shylock.
Shylock
I'll have my bond; speak not against my bond:
5 I have sworn an oath that I will have my bond.
Thou call'dst me dog before thou hadst a cause,
But, since I am a dog, beware my fangs:
The duke shall grant me justice. I do wonder,
Thou naughty gaoler, that thou art so fond
10 To come abroad with him at his request.
Antonio
I pray thee, hear me speak.
Shylock
I'll have my bond; I will not hear thee speak:
I'll have my bond, and therefore speak no more.
I'll not be made a soft and dull-eyed fool,
15 To shake the head, relent, and sigh, and yield
To Christian intercessors. Follow not;
I'll have no speaking; I will have my bond.   [*Exit*

18   *impenetrable*: hard-hearted.
19   *kept with*: lived among.

20   *follow*: appeal to.
     bootless: useless.

22   *deliver'd*: rescued.
     forfeitures: actions against those
who could not pay their debts;
Antonio himself is now enduring one
of these 'forfeitures'.
23   *made moan*: appealed.
25   Will never agree that Shylock
should be allowed to make his demand
(for the pound of flesh).
26   *the course of law*: that law must
take its course.
27-31   Because if 'the course of law' is
not allowed ('denied'), then the rights
('commodity') of foreigners
('strangers') will make them doubt
('impeach') Venetian justice; and this
will be a serious matter, because the
city's prosperity ('profit') depends on
international trade.
32   *so bated me*: made me lose so
much weight.
34   *bloody*: blood-thirsty.

Act 3   Scene 4
Portia asks Lorenzo to look after her
house until she and Nerissa return.
They are going to Venice, and plan to
dress as men to play a trick on their
husbands.

2   *conceit*: understanding.
3   *amity*: friendship.

5   *to whom*: i.e. Antonio.

7   *lover*: friend.
8-9   *you would . . . you*: you would be
more proud that you had done this
deed than you are of your usual acts of
kindness ('bounty').

Solanio
It is the most impenetrable cur
That ever kept with men.
Antonio   Let him alone:
20 I'll follow him no more with bootless prayers.
He seeks my life; his reason well I know.
I oft deliver'd from his forfeitures
Many that have at times made moan to me;
Therefore he hates me.
Solanio   I am sure the duke
25 Will never grant this forfeiture to hold.
Antonio
The duke cannot deny the course of law:
For the commodity that strangers have
With us in Venice, if it be denied,
Will much impeach the justice of the state,
30 Since that the trade and profit of the city
Consisteth of all nations. Therefore, go:
These griefs and losses have so bated me,
That I shall hardly spare a pound of flesh
Tomorrow to my bloody creditor.
35 Well, gaoler, on. Pray God, Bassanio come
To see me pay his debt, and then I care not!
                                    [*Exeunt*

Scene 4 *Belmont. A room in Portia's house*

Enter Portia, Nerissa, Lorenzo, Jessica,
and Balthazar
Lorenzo
Madam, although I speak it in your presence,
You have a noble and a true conceit
Of god-like amity; which appears most strongly
In bearing thus the absence of your lord.
5 But if you knew to whom you show this honour,
How true a gentleman you send relief,
How dear a lover of my lord your husband,
I know you would be prouder of the work
Than customary bounty can enforce you.

12   *waste*: spend.

13   Whose souls are joined together by the same bond of marriage (as oxen are joined by a yoke).

14   *be needs*: necessarily be.
a like: the same.

15   *lineaments*: characteristics.

17   *bosom lover*: close friend.

19   *bestow'd*: spent.

20   *the . . . soul*: Portia has argued that lovers must be like each other in soul, and that close friends must also resemble each other; therefore Antonio must be like Bassanio, whose soul resembles Portia's own.

22   *comes too near*: is too like.

25   *husbandry and manage*: careful management.

33   *deny*: refuse.
imposition: task.

37   *my mind*: what I intend.

38   *acknowledge*: recognize your authority.

44   *it back on you*: the same to you.

Portia
10 I never did repent for doing good,
   Nor shall not now: for in companions
   That do converse and waste the time together,
   Whose souls do bear an equal yoke of love,
   There must be needs a like proportion
15 Of lineaments, of manners, and of spirit;
   Which makes me think that this Antonio,
   Being the bosom lover of my lord,
   Must needs be like my lord. If it be so,
   How little is the cost I have bestow'd
20 In purchasing the semblance of my soul
   From out the state of hellish cruelty!
   This comes too near the praising of myself;
   Therefore, no more of it: hear other things.
   Lorenzo, I commit into your hands
25 The husbandry and manage of my house
   Until my lord's return: for mine own part,
   I have toward heaven breath'd a secret vow
   To live in prayer and contemplation,
   Only attended by Nerissa here,
30 Until her husband and my lord's return.
   There is a monastery two miles off,
   And there we will abide. I do desire you
   Not to deny this imposition,
   The which my love and some necessity
35 Now lays upon you.
    Lorenzo   Madam, with all my heart:
   I shall obey you in all fair commands.
    Portia
   My people do already know my mind,
   And will acknowledge you and Jessica
   In place of Lord Bassanio and myself.
40 So fare you well till we shall meet again.
    Lorenzo
   Fair thoughts and happy hours attend on you!
    Jessica
   I wish your ladyship all heart's content.
    Portia
   I thank you for your wish, and am well pleas'd
   To wish it back on you: fare you well, Jessica.
        [*Exeunt* Jessica *and* Lorenzo

46   *ever*: always.
      honest-true: honest and trust-
   worthy.
47   *So . . . still*: may I continue to
   find you so.
48   *all . . . man*: go as fast as a man
   can.
49   *render*: give.
51   *And look*: and take care of.
52   *imagin'd speed*: all conceivable
   speed.
53   *traject*: landing-place.
54   *trades*: carries passengers for
   hire.
56   *convenient speed*: as fast as I can.

57   *work in hand*: a plan in my mind.

59   *think of us*: expect to see us.

60   *habit*: costume.
61   *accomplished*: equipped.
62   *that we lack*: i.e. the attributes of
   masculinity.
      wager: bet.
63   *accoutered*: dressed up.
64   *prettier*: smarter.
66   *between . . . boy*: as though my
   voice were breaking (changing from a
   boy's voice to a man's voice).
67   *reed*: squeaky.
      mincing: dainty, lady-like.
68   *frays*: fights.
69   *bragging*: boastful.
      quaint: elaborate.
72   *I . . . withal*: I could not do anything about it.
74   *puny*: feeble, silly.
75-6 *I have . . . twelvemonth*: that it is
   a year since I left school.
77   *raw*: crude.
      jacks: fellows.
78   *turn to men*: change into men.
   Portia pretends to think that Nerissa
   means 'take men for lovers'.

45   Now, Balthazar,
     As I have ever found thee honest-true,
     So let me find thee still. Take this same letter,
     And use thou all th' endeavour of a man
     In speed to Padua: see thou render this
50   Into my cousin's hand, Doctor Bellario;
     And look what notes and garments he doth give
        thee,
     Bring them, I pray thee, with imagin'd speed
     Unto the traject, to the common ferry
     Which trades to Venice. Waste no time in words,
55   But get thee gone: I shall be there before thee.
        Balthazar
     Madam, I go with all convenient speed.   [*Exit*
        Portia
     Come on, Nerissa: I have work in hand
     That you yet know not of: we'll see our husbands
     Before they think of us.
        Nerissa   Shall they see us?
        Portia
60   They shall, Nerissa; but in such a habit
     That they shall think we are accomplished
     With that we lack. I'll hold thee any wager,
     When we are both accoutered like young men,
     I'll prove the prettier fellow of the two,
65   And wear my dagger with the braver grace,
     And speak between the change of man and boy
     With a reed voice, and turn two mincing steps
     Into a manly stride, and speak of frays
     Like a fine bragging youth, and tell quaint lies,
70   How honourable ladies sought my love,
     Which I denying, they fell sick and died—
     I could not do withal; then I'll repent,
     And wish, for all that, that I had not kill'd them.
     And twenty of these puny lies I'll tell,
75   That men shall swear I have discontinu'd school
     Above a twelvemonth. I have within my mind
     A thousand raw tricks of these bragging jacks,
     Which I will practise.
        Nerissa   Why, shall we turn to men?

80   *lewd interpreter*: someone with a dirty mind.
81   *device*: plan.

84   *measure*: travel.

Portia
80 Fie, what a question's that,
If thou wert near a lewd interpreter!
But come: I'll tell thee all my whole device
When I am in my coach, which stays for us
At the park gate; and therefore haste away,
For we must measure twenty miles today.

[*Exeunt*

Act 3   Scene 5
Launcelot Gobbo teases Jessica about her Jewish nationality. Her husband Lorenzo joins in the fun.

1   *look you*: you see.
     the sins of the father: Launcelot is quoting the first of the Ten Commandments (Exodus 20: 5).
2   *laid upon*: revenged upon.
3   *I fear you*: I fear for you.
     plain: honest.
4   *agitation*: Launcelot means 'cogitation' (= considered opinion).
7   *bastard hope*: both 'false hope' and 'hope that you are a bastard'.
7-8 *but . . . neither*: only.
10-11 *got you not*: did not beget you.
12   *so*: if that were the case.
13   *should . . . me*: I should be punished for.
15-16 *Scylla . . . Charybdis*: monsters of classical legend, taking the form of rocks and a whirlpool on either side of the straits between Italy and Sicily; sailors who escaped one were usually caught by the other.
17   *gone*: doomed.
18   Jessica refers to 1 Corinthians 7: 14: 'the unbelieving wife is sanctified by the husband'.
20-1 *we . . . before*: there were enough of us Christians before he converted you.
21   *e'en*: quite.
21-2 *one by another*: together.
22-3 *raise . . . hogs*: because as Christians they will be allowed to eat pork, which is forbidden to Jews.
24   *rasher on the coals*: slice of bacon cooking on the fire.
24-5 *for money*: at any price.

Scene 5 *Belmont. Portia's garden*

Enter Launcelot *and* Jessica

Launcelot
Yes, truly; for, look you, the sins of the father are to be laid upon the children; therefore, I promise you, I fear you. I was always plain with you, and so now I speak my agitation of the matter: therefore
5 be o' good cheer; for, truly, I think you are damned. There is but one hope in it that can do you any good, and that is but a kind of bastard hope neither.

Jessica
And what hope is that, I pray thee?

Launcelot
10 Marry, you may partly hope that your father got you not, that you are not the Jew's daughter.

Jessica
That were a kind of bastard hope, indeed: so the sins of my mother should be visited upon me.

Launcelot
Truly then I fear you are damned both by father
15 and mother: thus when I shun Scylla (your father) I fall into Charybdis (your mother): well, you are gone both ways.

Jessica
I shall be saved by my husband; he hath made me a Christian.

Launcelot
20 Truly the more to blame he: we were Christians enow before; e'en as many as could well live one by another. This making of Christians will raise the price of hogs: if we grow all to be pork-eaters, we shall not shortly have a rasher on the coals for
25 money.

Enter Lorenzo

Jessica

I'll tell my husband, Launcelot, what you say: here he comes.

Lorenzo

I shall grow jealous of you shortly, Launcelot, if you thus get my wife into corners.

Jessica

30 Nay, you need not fear us, Lorenzo: Launcelot and I are out. He tells me flatly there's no mercy for me in heaven, because I am a Jew's daughter: and he says you are no good member of the commonwealth, for, in converting Jews to Christians, you
35 raise the price of pork.

Lorenzo

I shall answer that better to the commonwealth than you can the getting up of the negro's belly: the Moor is with child by you, Launcelot.

Launcelot

It is much that the Moor should be more than
40 reason; but if she be less than an honest woman, she is indeed more than I took her for.

Lorenzo

How every fool can play upon the word! I think the best grace of wit will shortly turn into silence, and discourse grow commendable in none only but
45 parrots. Go in, sirrah: bid them prepare for dinner.

Launcelot

That is done, sir; they have all stomachs.

Lorenzo

Goodly Lord, what a wit-snapper are you! then bid them prepare dinner.

Launcelot

That is done too, sir; only 'cover' is the word.

Lorenzo

50 Will you cover, then, sir?

Launcelot

Not so, sir, neither; I know my duty.

Lorenzo

Yet more quarrelling with occasion! Wilt thou show the whole wealth of thy wit in an instant? I pray thee, understand a plain man in his plain

29   *into corners*: i.e. where you can whisper together, and flirt.

31   *are out*: have fallen out, have quarrelled.
       flatly: certainly.

37   *getting up*: swelling.
38   *Moor*: Moorish (woman); Launcelot's reply puns on 'Moor' and 'more'.
39–40 *more than reason*: bigger than she ought to be.
40–1   *but if . . . for*: even if she is not quite an honest woman, she is nevertheless better than I thought her to be (presumably he thought she was a whore).
43   *the best . . . silence*: soon, the best way to show one's cleverness will be by keeping silent.
44–5   *discourse . . . parrots*: talking will be something to admire only in parrots.
46   *they have all stomachs*: they are all hungry (with a pun on 'stomachs' = appetites, and = digestions).
47   *wit-snapper*: comedian.
49   *'cover' is the word*: you ought to say 'lay the table'; but when Lorenzo does use the word 'cover', Launcelot pretends to think he intends another meaning—'put on your hat'.
51   *my duty*: respect; inferiors stood bare-headed in the presence of their superiors.
52   *quarrelling with occasion*: taking every opportunity to make a play on words.

55 meaning: go to thy fellows; bid them cover the
table, serve in the meat, and we will come in to
dinner.

Launcelot

For the table, sir, it shall be served in; for the meat,
sir, it shall be covered; for your coming in to dinner,
60 sir, why, let it be as humours and conceits shall
govern.   [*Exit*

Lorenzo

O dear discretion, how his words are suited!
The fool hath planted in his memory
An army of good words, and I do know
65 A many fools, that stand in better place,
Garnish'd like him, that for a tricksy word
Defy the matter. How cheer'st thou, Jessica?
And now, good sweet, say thy opinion;
How dost thou like the Lord Bassanio's wife?

Jessica

70 Past all expressing. It is very meet
The Lord Bassanio live an upright life,
For, having such a blessing in his lady,
He finds the joys of heaven here on earth;
And if on earth he do not merit it,
75 In reason he should never come to heaven.
Why, if two gods should play some heavenly match,
And on the wager lay two earthly women,
And Portia one, there must be something else
Pawn'd with the other, for the poor rude world
80 Hath not her fellow.

Lorenzo   Even such a husband
Hast thou of me, as she is for a wife.

Jessica

Nay, but ask my opinion too of that.

Lorenzo

I will anon; first, let us go to dinner.

Jessica

Nay, let me praise you while I have a stomach.

Lorenzo

85 No, pray thee, let it serve for table-talk;
Then howsome'er thou speak'st, 'mong other
things
I shall digest it.

Jessica   Well, I'll set you forth.
                                             [*Exeunt*

---

58   *For the table*: as far as the food is
concerned (Launcelot pretends to
mistake Lorenzo's 'table').

59   *covered*: i.e. to keep it hot.

60–1 *as . . . govern*: as your whims and
fancies please you.

62   *O dear . . . suited*: Lorenzo
laughs at Launcelot's ability to dis-
tinguish different meanings of a word,
and fit them for his purpose.

65   *A many*: a lot of.
stand in better place: have better
positions (perhaps as professional
fools).

66   *Garnish'd*: supplied with a stock
of words; perhaps Lorenzo also refers
to the extra gold braid on Launcelot's
livery (see 2, 2, 149) which makes him
look like a court jester.
tricksy: clever.

67   *Defy the matter*: confuse the
sense of what they are saying.
How cheer'st thou: are you
happy?

70   *Past all expressing*: I can't find
words to say how good she is.
meet: necessary.

71   *upright*: honourable.

75   *In reason*: it is only reasonable
that.

77–80 If each of these gods should give
a human woman as his bet ('wager'),
and one of these women was Portia,
something else would have to be
gambled ('Pawn'd') with the other
woman, for no woman in the world is
Portia's equal ('fellow').

83   *anon*: shortly.

84   *stomach*: both 'appetite for
dinner' and 'desire to praise you'.

85   *table-talk*: conversation during
the meal.

86   *howsome'er*: however.

87   *set you forth*: put you in your
place.

Act 4

Act 4 Scene 1

The Duke asks Shylock to show mercy
to Antonio, but Shylock refuses and
insists on having his pound of flesh.
A young lawyer comes into the court—
it is Portia in disguise, with Nerissa as
the lawyer's clerk. Portia makes a
speech in praise of mercy, but Shylock
is unmoved. Portia agrees that he is
legally entitled to a pound of Antonio's
flesh, and Antonio prepares to die. At
the last moment Portia finds a way of
escape for Antonio. Bassanio is very
grateful because his friend's life has
been saved, and he offers to reward
the young lawyer. Portia asks for a
ring.

5   *void*: empty.
6   *dram*: a tiny measure.
7   *qualify*: moderate.
8   *stands obdurate*: remains hard-
hearted.

11   *arm'd*: prepared.

Scene 1 *Venice. A court of justice*

Enter the Duke, *the* Merchants, Antonio,
Bassanio, Gratiano, Salerio, *and* Officers
of the Court

Duke
What, is Antonio here?

Antonio
Ready, so please your Grace.

Duke
I am sorry for thee: thou art come to answer
A stony adversary, an inhuman wretch
5 Uncapable of pity, void and empty
From any dram of mercy.

Antonio   I have heard
Your Grace hath ta'en great pains to qualify
His rigorous course; but since he stands obdurate,
And that no lawful means can carry me
10 Out of his envy's reach, I do oppose
My patience to his fury, and am arm'd
To suffer with a quietness of spirit
The very tyranny and rage of his.

Duke
Go one, and call the Jew into the court.

Salerio
15 He is ready at the door: he comes, my lord.

Enter Shylock

Duke
Make room, and let him stand before our face.
Shylock, the world thinks, and I think so too,
That thou but lead'st this fashion of thy malice
To the last hour of act; and then 'tis thought
20 Thou'lt show thy mercy and remorse more strange
Than is thy strange apparent cruelty;
And where thou now exact'st the penalty—
Which is a pound of this poor merchant's flesh—
Thou wilt not only loose the forfeiture,
25 But, touch'd with human gentleness and love,
Forgive a moiety of the principal,
Glancing an eye of pity on his losses,
That have of late so huddled on his back,
Enow to press a royal merchant down,
30 And pluck commiseration of his state
From brassy bosoms and rough hearts of flints,
From stubborn Turks and Tartars, never train'd
To offices of tender courtesy.
We all expect a gentle answer, Jew.

Shylock
35 I have possess'd your Grace of what I purpose;
And by our holy Sabbath have I sworn
To have the due and forfeit of my bond:
If you deny it, let the danger light
Upon your charter and your city's freedom.
40 You'll ask me, why I rather choose to have
A weight of carrion flesh than to receive
Three thousand ducats. I'll not answer that,
But say it is my humour. Is it answer'd?
What if my house be troubled with a rat,
45 And I be pleas'd to give ten thousand ducats
To have it ban'd? What, are you answer'd yet?
Some men there are love not a gaping pig;
Some, that are mad if they behold a cat;
And others, when the bagpipe sings i' the nose,
50 Cannot contain their urine: for affection,
Master of passion, sways it to the mood
Of what it likes, or loathes. Now, for your answer:
As there is no firm reason to be render'd,

18-19   *thou . . . act*: you intend to carry on with this show of cruelty until the last moment.
20   *more strange*: which will be more strange.
21   *apparent*: as it appears now.
22   *exact'st*: insist on having.
24   *loose the forfeiture*: refuse to accept the penalty that Antonio should pay.
26   Allow him to keep a part of the original sum he borrowed.
29   *Enow*: enough.
        royal: noble.
30   *commiseration of*: sympathy for.
31   *brassy bosoms*: hearts as hard as brass.
32   *stubborn*: unfeeling.
32-3   *train'd . . . courtesy*: taught to behave with gentleness.
35   *possess'd*: informed.
36   *Sabbath*: the seventh day of the Jewish week, which was the holiest day (Genesis 2: 3).
37   *due . . . bond*: the proper penalty for not repaying my loan.
38   *light*: descend.
39   *charter*: the document by which Venice was granted independence ('freedom').
41   *carrion*: rotten.
43   *it is my humour*: because I want it.
46   *ban'd*: poisoned.
47   *a gaping pig*: a pig's head, roasted, with the mouth open.
49   *sings i' the nose*: drones.
50-2   *affection . . . loathes*: prejudice is stronger than any emotion ('passion'), and directs our emotion to love or hate the objects of our prejudice.

54-6   *he ... he ... he*: this man ... that man ... the other man.

56   *woollen bagpipe*: the bag of the pipes was covered in woollen material.

56-8   *but ... offended*: but when he is himself offended, he is compelled (forced) to react in such a shameful way that he must give offence to others.

60   *lodg'd*: deep-rooted.

62   *A losing suit*: a legal case where I must lose money.

64   *current*: outpouring.

68   A single offence is not a cause for hatred.

70   *think ... Jew*: remember that you are arguing with the Jew.

72   *main flood*: ocean tide.
     bate: reduce.

73   *use question with*: ask.

76   *wag*: wave.

77   *fretten*: blown.

82   But as quickly and simply as you can.

87   *draw*: accept.

Why he cannot abide a gaping pig;
55 Why he, a harmless necessary cat;
Why he, a woollen bagpipe, but of force
Must yield to such inevitable shame
As to offend, himself being offended;
So can I give no reason, nor I will not,
60 More than a lodg'd hate and a certain loathing
I bear Antonio, that I follow thus
A losing suit against him. Are you answer'd?
  Bassanio
This is no answer, thou unfeeling man,
To excuse the current of thy cruelty.
  Shylock
65 I am not bound to please thee with my answers.
  Bassanio
Do all men kill the things they do not love?
  Shylock
Hates any man the thing he would not kill?
  Bassanio
Every offence is not a hate at first.
  Shylock
What! wouldst thou have a serpent sting thee twice?
  Antonio
70 I pray you, think you question with the Jew:
You may as well go stand upon the beach,
And bid the main flood bate his usual height;
You may as well use question with the wolf,
Why he hath made the ewe bleat for the lamb;
75 You may as well forbid the mountain pines
To wag their high tops, and to make no noise
When they are fretten with the gusts of heaven;
You may as well do anything most hard,
As seek to soften that—than which what's harder?—
80 His Jewish heart: therefore, I do beseech you,
Make no more offers, use no farther means;
But with all brief and plain conveniency,
Let me have judgment, and the Jew his will.
  Bassanio
For thy three thousand ducats here is six.
  Shylock
85 If every ducat in six thousand ducats
Were in six parts, and every part a ducat,
I would not draw them. I would have my bond.

Duke
How shalt thou hope for mercy, rendering none?
Shylock
What judgment shall I dread, doing no wrong?
90 You have among you many a purchas'd slave,
Which, like your asses and your dogs and mules,
You use in abject and in slavish parts,
Because you bought them: shall I say to you,
'Let them be free, marry them to your heirs?
95 Why sweat they under burdens? let their beds
Be made as soft as yours, and let their palates
Be season'd with such viands?' You will answer,
'The slaves are ours'. So do I answer you:
The pound of flesh which I demand of him,
100 Is dearly bought; 'tis mine and I will have it.
If you deny me, fie upon your law!
There is no force in the decrees of Venice.
I stand for judgment. Answer—shall I have it?
Duke
Upon my power I may dismiss this court,
105 Unless Bellario, a learned doctor,
Whom I have sent for to determine this,
Come here today.
Salerio   My lord, here stays without
A messenger with letters from the doctor,
New come from Padua.
Duke
110 Bring us the letters: call the messenger.
Bassanio
Good cheer, Antonio! What, man, courage yet!
The Jew shall have my flesh, blood, bones, and all,
Ere thou shalt lose for me one drop of blood.
Antonio
I am a tainted wether of the flock,
115 Meetest for death: the weakest kind of fruit
Drops earliest to the ground; and so let me.
You cannot better be employ'd, Bassanio,
Than to live still, and write mine epitaph.

Enter Nerissa, *dressed like a lawyer's clerk*
Duke
Came you from Padua, from Bellario?

90 *purchas'd slave*: slave that you have bought.
92 *in abject . . . parts*: for lowly and servile tasks.
97 *Be season'd . . . viands*: be treated with the same food as your own.
101 *fie*: shame.
102 *force*: power.
104 *Upon my power*: with my authority.
107 *stays without*: waits outside.
114 *tainted wether*: diseased ram.
115 *Meetest*: most suitable.
118 *live still*: go on living.

Nerissa
120 From both, my lord. Bellario greets your Grace.
                    [*Presents a letter*

Bassanio
Why dost thou whet thy knife so earnestly?

Shylock
To cut the forfeiture from that bankrupt there.

Gratiano
Not on thy sole, but on thy soul, harsh Jew,
Thou mak'st thy knife keen; but no metal can,
125 No, not the hangman's axe, bear half the keenness
Of thy sharp envy. Can no prayers pierce thee?

Shylock
No, none that thou hast wit enough to make.

Gratiano
O, be thou damn'd, inexorable dog!
And for thy life let justice be accus'd.
130 Thou almost mak'st me waver in my faith
To hold opinion with Pythagoras,
That souls of animals infuse themselves
Into the trunks of men: thy currish spirit
Govern'd a wolf, who, hang'd for human slaughter,
135 Even from the gallows did his fell soul fleet,
And whilst thou lay'st in thy unhallow'd dam,
Infus'd itself in thee; for thy desires
Are wolvish, bloody, starv'd, and ravenous.

Shylock
Till thou canst rail the seal from off my bond.
140 Thou but offend'st thy lungs to speak so loud:
Repair thy wit, good youth, or it will fall
To cureless ruin. I stand here for law.

Duke
This letter from Bellario doth commend
A young and learned doctor to our court.
145 Where is he?

Nerissa   He attendeth here hard by,
To know your answer, whether you'll admit him.

Duke
With all my heart: some three or four of you
Go give him courteous conduct to this place.
                    [*Exeunt* Officers
Meantime, the court shall hear Bellario's letter.

---

121 *whet*: sharpen. Bassanio's comment in line 123 shows that Shylock is using the sole of his shoe for sharpening the knife.

128 *inexorable*: relentless.
129 Let justice be said to be guilty that you are alive.
131 *hold opinion*: agree.
   Pythagoras: a Greek philosopher who believed (as Bassanio explains) that the souls of men and of animals passed into other bodies.
132 *infuse*: pour.
133 *currish*: like a cur—a mongrel dog.
134 *hang'd for human slaughter*: this was in fact a means of destroying killer animals.
135 *Even*: directly.
   fell: cruel.
   fleet: speed away.
136 *unhallow'd*: unsanctified (because non-Christian).
   dam: mother.
139 *rail*: shout.
140 *offend'st*: trouble.
142 *cureless*: incurable.
145 *hard*: near.
148 *give him courteous conduct*: lead him politely.

150 *Your Grace shall understand that at the receipt of*
your letter I am very sick; but in the instant that your
messenger came, in loving visitation was with me a
young doctor of Rome; his name is Balthazar.
I acquainted him with the cause in controversy
155 *between the Jew and Antonio the merchant. We*
turned o'er many books together. He is furnished with
my opinion; which, bettered with his own learning—
the greatness whereof I cannot enough commend—
comes with him, at my importunity, to fill up your
160 *Grace's request in my stead. I beseech you, let his lack*
of years be no impediment to let him lack a reverend
estimation, for I never knew so young a body with so
old a head. I leave him to your gracious acceptance,
whose trial shall better publish his commendation.

Enter Portia, *dressed like a doctor of law*

165 You hear the learn'd Bellario, what he writes:
And here, I take it, is the doctor come.
Give me your hand. Come you from old Bellario?

Portia
I did, my lord.

Duke   You are welcome: take your place.
Are you acquainted with the difference
170 That holds this present question in the court?

Portia
I am informed throughly of the cause.
Which is the merchant here, and which the Jew?

Duke
Antonio and old Shylock, both stand forth.

Portia
Is your name Shylock?

Shylock   Shylock is my name.

Portia
175 Of a strange nature is the suit you follow;
Yet in such rule, that the Venetian law
Cannot impugn you as you do proceed.
[*To* Antonio] You stand within his danger, do you
   not?

Antonio
Ay, so he says.

Portia   Do you confess the bond?

Antonio
180 I do.

---

154   *cause*: matter.
       controversy: dispute.

156   *turned o'er*: looked through.
       is furnished: has been given.

157   *bettered*: improved.

159   *importunity*: earnest request.

160   *in my stead*: instead of me.

160-2   *let . . . estimation*: do not think
       poorly of him because he is young.

164   *whose . . . commendation*: try him,
       and you will see how much better he is
       than my praise.

169-70   *the difference . . . court*: the
       dispute that is at present on trial in
       this court.

171   *throughly*: thoroughly.

176   *in such rule*: so correctly.

177   Cannot find any fault in your
       proceedings.

178   *within his danger*: in danger from
       him.

Portia   Then must the Jew be merciful.

Shylock

On what compulsion must I? tell me that.

Portia

The quality of mercy is not strain'd;
It droppeth as the gentle rain from heaven
Upon the place beneath: it is twice bless'd;

185 It blesseth him that gives and him that takes.
'Tis mightiest in the mightiest: it becomes
The throned monarch better than his crown;
His sceptre shows the force of temporal power,
The attribute to awe and majesty,

190 Wherein doth sit the dread and fear of kings:
But mercy is above this sceptred sway,
It is enthroned in the hearts of kings,
It is an attribute to God himself,
And earthly power doth then show likest God's

195 When mercy seasons justice. Therefore, Jew,
Though justice be thy plea, consider this,
That in the course of justice none of us
Should see salvation: we do pray for mercy,
And that same prayer doth teach us all to render

200 The deeds of mercy. I have spoke thus much
To mitigate the justice of thy plea,
Which if thou follow, this strict court of Venice
Must needs give sentence 'gainst the merchant
     there.

Shylock

My deeds upon my head! I crave the law,

205 The penalty and forfeit of my bond.

Portia

Is he not able to discharge the money?

Bassanio

Yes, here I tender it for him in the court;
Yea, twice the sum: if that will not suffice,
I will be bound to pay it ten times o'er,

210 On forfeit of my hands, my head, my heart.
If this will not suffice, it must appear
That malice bears down truth. And, I beseech you,
Wrest once the law to your authority:
To do a great right, do a little wrong,

215 And curb this cruel devil of his will.

181   *On . . . I*: what will compel me
and force me to do it?

182   *is not strain'd*: cannot be forced
(constrained).

186   *'Tis . . . mightiest*: both 'mercy
is seen at its most powerful in the men
with most power', and 'mercy is the
most powerful weapon that the most
powerful men possess'.
     becomes: suits.

188-9 The king's sceptre symbolizes
his earthly ('temporal') power, which is
the proper characteristic ('attribute') of
a royal man ('majesty') who commands
respect ('awe').

191   *this sceptred sway*: this world that
is ruled by men with sceptres.

193   *attribute to*: quality belonging to.

195   *seasons*: moderates.

196   *Though . . . plea*: although you
are asking for justice.

197-8 *in . . . salvation*: if we were all to
get what we deserve, in the strict
course of justice none of us would be
saved.

201   To ask you to soften your
demand for justice.

203   *Must needs*: is compelled.

204   *My . . . head*: I will take the
responsibility for what I am doing.
     crave: ask for.

206   *discharge*: repay.

207   *tender*: offer.

209   *be bound*: make a legal promise.

212   *bears down*: overcomes.

213   *Wrest*: twist.
     once: on this one occasion.
     to: with.

215   *curb*: restrain.

Portia
It must not be. There is no power in Venice
Can alter a decree established:
'Twill be recorded for a precedent,
And many an error by the same example
220 Will rush into the state. It cannot be.

Shylock
A Daniel come to judgment! yea, a Daniel!
O wise young judge, how I do honour thee!

Portia
I pray you, let me look upon the bond.

Shylock
Here 'tis, most reverend doctor, here it is.

Portia
225 Shylock, there's thrice thy money offer'd thee.

Shylock
An oath, an oath, I have an oath in heaven;
Shall I lay perjury upon my soul?
No, not for Venice.

Portia   Why, this bond is forfeit;
And lawfully by this the Jew may claim
230 A pound of flesh, to be by him cut off
Nearest the merchant's heart. Be merciful:
Take thrice thy money; bid me tear the bond.

Shylock
When it is paid according to the tenour.
It doth appear you are a worthy judge;
235 You know the law, your exposition
Hath been most sound: I charge you by the law,
Whereof you are a well-deserving pillar,
Proceed to judgment: by my soul I swear
There is no power in the tongue of man
240 To alter me. I stay here on my bond.

Most heartily I do beseech the court
To give the judgment.

Portia   Why then, thus it is:
You must prepare your bosom for his knife.

Shylock
O noble judge! O excellent young man!

Portia
245 For, the intent and purpose of the law

221   *Daniel*: the 'History of Susanna' in the Apocrypha tells how God sent Daniel, 'a young youth', to give judgement against the elders.

233   *tenour*: actual wording.

235   *exposition*: understanding of the case.

237   *pillar*: support.

241   *Most heartily*: with all my heart.

246   *Hath full relation*: entirely
supports.

249   *elder*: more mature.

253   *balance*: scales.
255   *on your charge*: at your expense.
257   *nominated*: specified.

262   *arm'd*: i.e. spiritually.

266   *still her use*: usually her custom.

273   *speak . . . death*: speak kindly of
me when I am dead.

276   *Repent but you*: you must only
regret.

Hath full relation to the penalty,
Which here appeareth due upon the bond.
        Shylock
'Tis very true! O wise and upright judge!
How much more elder art thou than thy looks!
        Portia
250 Therefore lay bare your bosom.
        Shylock   Ay, 'his breast':
So says the bond:—doth it not, noble judge?—
'Nearest his heart'—those are the very words.
        Portia
It is so. Are there balance here to weigh
The flesh?
        Shylock   I have them ready.
        Portia
255 Have by some surgeon, Shylock, on your charge,
To stop his wounds, lest he do bleed to death.
        Shylock
Is it so nominated in the bond?
        Portia
It is not so express'd; but what of that?
'Twere good you do so much for charity.
        Shylock
260 I cannot find it: 'tis not in the bond.
        Portia
You, merchant, have you anything to say?
        Antonio
But little: I am arm'd and well prepar'd.
Give me your hand, Bassanio: fare you well!
Grieve not that I am fall'n to this for you,
265 For herein Fortune shows herself more kind
Than is her custom: it is still her use
To let the wretched man outlive his wealth,
To view with hollow eye and wrinkled brow
An age of poverty; from which lingering penance
270 Of such misery doth she cut me off.
Commend me to your honourable wife.
Tell her the process of Antonio's end;
Say how I lov'd you, speak me fair in death;
And, when the tale is told, bid her be judge
275 Whether Bassanio had not once a love.
Repent but you that you shall lose your friend,

And he repents not that he pays your debt;
For if the Jew do cut but deep enough,
I'll pay it instantly with all my heart.

Bassanio

281   *Which*: who.

280 Antonio, I am married to a wife
Which is as dear to me as life itself;
But life itself, my wife, and all the world,
Are not with me esteem'd above thy life:

285   *deliver*: save.

285 Here to this devil, to deliver you.

Portia

Your wife would give you little thanks for that,
If she were by to hear you make the offer.

Gratiano

I have a wife, who, I protest, I love:
I would she were in heaven, so she could

290 Entreat some power to change this currish Jew.

Nerissa

'Tis well you offer it behind her back;
The wish would make else an unquiet house.

Shylock

These be the Christian husbands! I have a
daughter;

294   *stock*: breed.
      Barabas: the thief who was
released when Christ was crucified
(St. John 18: 40).
296   *trifle time*: waste time in
trivialities.
      pursue: go on with.

Would any of the stock of Barabas
295 Had been her husband rather than a Christian!
We trifle time; I pray thee, pursue sentence.

Portia

A pound of that same merchant's flesh is thine:
The court awards it, and the law doth give it.

Shylock

Most rightful judge!

Portia

300 And you must cut this flesh from off his breast:
The law allows it, and the court awards it.

Shylock

Most learned judge! A sentence! come, prepare!

Portia

303   *Tarry*: wait.
304   *jot*: drop.

Tarry a little: there is something else.
This bond doth give thee here no jot of blood;
305 The words expressly are 'a pound of flesh':
Take then thy bond, take thou thy pound of flesh;

But, in the cutting it, if thou dost shed
One drop of Christian blood, thy lands and goods
Are, by the laws of Venice, confiscate
310 Unto the state of Venice.

Gratiano
O upright judge! Mark, Jew: O learned judge!

Shylock
Is that the law?

Portia   Thyself shalt see the act;
For, as thou urgest justice, be assur'd
Thou shalt have justice more than thou desir'st.

Gratiano
315 O learned judge! Mark, Jew: a learned judge!

Shylock
I take this offer then: pay the bond thrice,
And let the Christian go.

Bassanio   Here is the money.

Portia
Soft!
The Jew shall have all justice; soft! no haste:—
320 He shall have nothing but the penalty.

Gratiano
O Jew! an upright judge, a learned judge!

Portia
Therefore prepare thee to cut off the flesh.
Shed thou no blood; nor cut thou less, nor more,
But just a pound of flesh: if thou tak'st more,
325 Or less, than a just pound, be it but so much
As makes it light or heavy in the substance,
Or the division of the twentieth part
Of one poor scruple, nay, if the scale do turn
But in the estimation of a hair,
330 Thou diest, and all thy goods are confiscate.

Gratiano
A second Daniel, a Daniel, Jew!
Now, infidel, I have you on the hip.

Portia
Why doth the Jew pause? take thy forfeiture.

Shylock
Give me my principal, and let me go.

Bassanio
335 I have it ready for thee; here it is.

312 *act*: the legal act confirming the law.
313 *urgest*: demand.

321 *upright*: honest.

326 *substance*: weight.

328 *scruple*: a weight unit (used by the old apothecaries) of 20 grains.
329 *estimation*: weight.

332 *on the hip*: at my mercy.

334 *principal*: the original sum borrowed.

Portia
He hath refus'd it in the open court:
He shall have merely justice, and his bond.
Gratiano
A Daniel, still say I; a second Daniel!
I thank thee, Jew, for teaching me that word.
Shylock
340 Shall I not have barely my principal?
Portia
Thou shalt have nothing but the forfeiture,
To be so taken at thy peril, Jew.
Shylock
Why, then the devil give him good of it!
I'll stay no longer question.
Portia   Tarry, Jew:
345 The law hath yet another hold on you.
It is enacted in the laws of Venice,
If it be prov'd against an alien
That by direct or indirect attempts
He seek the life of any citizen,
350 The party 'gainst the which he doth contrive
Shall seize one half his goods; the other half
Comes to the privy coffer of the state;
And the offender's life lies in the mercy
Of the duke only, 'gainst all other voice.
355 In which predicament, I say, thou stand'st;
For it appears by manifest proceeding,
That indirectly, and directly too,
Thou hast contriv'd against the very life
Of the defendant; and thou hast incurr'd
360 The danger formerly by me rehears'd.
Down therefore and beg mercy of the duke.
Gratiano
Beg that thou may'st have leave to hang thyself—
And yet, thy wealth being forfeit to the state,
Thou hast not left the value of a cord;
365 Therefore thou must be hang'd at the state's charge.
Duke
That thou shalt see the difference of our spirit,
I pardon thee thy life before thou ask it.
For half thy wealth, it is Antonio's;
The other half comes to the general state,
370 Which humbleness may drive unto a fine.

344   *question*: to argue.

346   *enacted*: decreed.

350   *party*: person (Portia uses the correct legal term, still used today).
       contrive: plot.
352   *privy coffer*: treasury.

354   *'gainst all other voice*: no matter what anyone else says.

356   *manifest proceeding*: quite clearly from what has happened.

360   *rehears'd*: declared.

369   *general state*: general use of the state.
370   And if you are humble this may be reduced to a fine.

371   *not for Antonio*: the money due
to Antonio will not be reduced.

377   *halter*: rope to hang himself with.
gratis: free of interest.

378   *So please*: if it pleases.

379   *quit*: be satisfied with.
for: instead of.

380   *so*: if.

381   *in use*: on trust—to use as
Antonio now describes.

385   *presently*: immediately.

387   *all he dies possess'd*: all that he
owns when he dies.

389   *recant*: withdraw.

396   *god-fathers*: these take the
responsibility for seeing that the
baptized child is properly educated in
the Christian faith; 'god-fathers' was
also a joking name for the members of
a jury—a body of twelve men who
were needed to pass sentence on a
criminal. Gratiano suggests that a jury
would have condemned Shylock to
death.

Portia
Ay, for the state; not for Antonio.
        Shylock
Nay, take my life and all; pardon not that:
You take my house, when you do take the prop
That doth sustain my house; you take my life
375 When you do take the means whereby I live.
        Portia
What mercy can you render him, Antonio?
        Gratiano
A halter gratis; nothing else, for God's sake!
        Antonio
So please my lord the duke, and all the court,
To quit the fine for one half of his goods,
380 I am content so he will let me have
The other half in use, to render it,
Upon his death, unto the gentleman
That lately stole his daughter.
Two things provided more, that, for this favour,
385 He presently become a Christian;
The other, that he do record a gift,
Here in the court, of all he dies possess'd,
Unto his son Lorenzo and his daughter.
        Duke
He shall do this, or else I do recant
390 The pardon that I late pronounced here.
        Portia
Art thou contented, Jew? what dost thou say?
        Shylock
I am content.
        Portia   Clerk, draw a deed of gift.
        Shylock
I pray you give me leave to go from hence:
I am not well. Send the deed after me,
395 And I will sign it.
        Duke   Get thee gone, but do it.
        Gratiano
In christening shalt thou have two god-fathers;
Had I been judge, thou shouldst have had ten more,
To bring thee to the gallows, not to the font.
                        [*Exit* Shylock
        Duke
Sir, I entreat you home with me to dinner.

402   *meet*: necessary.

403   *your leisure serves you not*: you do not have time to spare.
404   *gratify*: show your gratitude to.
405   *bound*: indebted.

408   *in lieu whereof*: in payment for this.

410   *freely*: most willingly.
      cope: reward.
      pains: trouble.
411   *over and above*: in addition.

416   *mercenary*: interested in money.
417   *know*: recognize.

419   *of force*: it is necessary.
      attempt you further: try harder to persuade you.
420   *some remembrance*: something to remind you.
      tribute: token of respect.
422   Not to refuse my request, and to forgive me for making it.
423   *You press me far*: you are very insistent.
424   *for your sake*: to acknowledge your politeness.
425   *for your love*: to acknowledge your love.

431   And now I really do want it.

Portia
400 I humbly do desire your Grace of pardon:
    I must away this night toward Padua,
    And it is meet I presently set forth.
    Duke
    I am sorry that your leisure serves you not.
    Antonio, gratify this gentleman,
405 For, in my mind, you are much bound to him.

[*Exeunt* Duke, Merchants, *and* Officers of the Court

    Bassanio
    Most worthy gentleman, I and my friend
    Have by your wisdom been this day acquitted
    Of grievous penalties, in lieu whereof,
    Three thousand ducats, due unto the Jew,
410 We freely cope your courteous pains withal.
    Antonio
    And stand indebted, over and above,
    In love and service to you evermore.
    Portia
    He is well paid that is well satisfied,
    And I, delivering you, am satisfied,
415 And therein do account myself well paid:
    My mind was never yet more mercenary.
    I pray you, know me when we meet again:
    I wish you well, and so I take my leave.
    Bassanio
    Dear sir, of force I must attempt you further:
420 Take some remembrance of us as a tribute,
    Not as a fee. Grant me two things, I pray you,
    Not to deny me, and to pardon me.
    Portia
    You press me far, and therefore I will yield.
    Give me your gloves, I'll wear them for your sake;
425 And (for your love) I'll take this ring from you.
    Do not draw back your hand; I'll take no more,
    And you in love shall not deny me this.
    Bassanio
    This ring, good sir? alas! it is a trifle,
    I will not shame myself to give you this.
    Portia
430 I will have nothing else but only this;
    And now methinks I have a mind to it.

Bassanio
There's more depends on this than on the value.
The dearest ring in Venice will I give you,
And find it out by proclamation:
435 Only for this, I pray you, pardon me.
Portia
I see, sir, you are liberal in offers:
You taught me first to beg, and now methinks
You teach me how a beggar should be answer'd.
Bassanio
Good sir, this ring was given me by my wife,
440 And, when she put it on, she made me vow
That I should neither sell, nor give, nor lose it.
Portia
That 'scuse serves many men to save their gifts.
And if your wife be not a mad-woman,
And know how well I have deserv'd this ring,
445 She would not hold out enemy for ever,
For giving it to me. Well, peace be with you.
                                    [*Exeunt* Portia *and* Nerissa
Antonio
My Lord Bassanio, let him have the ring:
Let his deservings and my love withal
Be valu'd 'gainst your wife's commandèment.
Bassanio
450 Go, Gratiano; run and overtake him;
Give him the ring, and bring him, if thou canst,
Unto Antonio's house. Away, make haste.
                                    [*Exit* Gratiano
Come, you and I will thither presently,
And in the morning early will we both
455 Fly toward Belmont. Come, Antonio.   [*Exeunt*

Scene 2 *Venice. A street*

Enter Portia *and* Nerissa
Portia
Inquire the Jew's house out, give him this deed,
And let him sign it. We'll away tonight,
And be a day before our husbands home:
This deed will be well welcome to Lorenzo.

434   *by proclamation*: by public announcement that I will buy the most expensive ring in Venice.
435   *for this*: i.e. this ring.
436   *liberal in offers*: generous only in making offers (not in fulfilling them).

442   *'scuse*: excuse.

445   *hold out enemy*: be angry with you.

449   *'gainst*: more highly than.
      commandèment: the extra *è* is for the sake of the rhythm.

Act 4   Scene 2
Gratiano gives Bassanio's ring to Portia, who is still disguised as the young lawyer and accompanied by Nerissa as her 'clerk'. Nerissa plans to get her own ring from Gratiano.
1   *Inquire . . . out*: find out where the Jew's house is.
      this deed: the document in which he promises to make Lorenzo his heir.

Enter Gratiano

Gratiano

5 Fair sir, you are well o'erta'en.

My Lord Bassanio, upon more advice,

Hath sent you here this ring, and doth entreat

Your company at dinner.

Portia   That cannot be.

His ring I do accept most thankfully,

10 And so, I pray you, tell him: furthermore,

I pray you, show my youth old Shylock's house.

Gratiano

That will I do.

Nerissa   Sir, I would speak with you.

[*Aside to* Portia] I'll see if I can get my husband's

ring.

Which I did make him swear to keep for ever.

Portia

15 Thou may'st, I warrant. We shall have old swearing

That they did give the rings away to men;

But we'll outface them, and outswear them too.

Away, make haste! thou know'st where I will tarry.

Nerissa

Come, good sir, will you show me to this house?

[*Exeunt*

6   *upon more advice*: having thought more about the matter.

15   *Thou may'st, I warrant*: I'm sure you will be able to do it.
old: a lot of.

18   *tarry*: wait.

Act 5

Act 5 Scene 1

Lorenzo and Jessica talk lovingly in
the moonlight. Messages are brought,
telling them that Portia and Bassanio
are (separately) on their way home.
After a short time, Portia and Nerissa
arrive at Belmont; a little later, as day
breaks, Bassanio and Gratiano appear.
The wives ask their husbands for the
rings, and pretend to be angry; at last
they reveal the truth.

4   *Troilus*: in the Trojan War,
Troilus was separated from his love,
Cressida, when she was taken into the
enemy (Greek) camp. Shakespeare
wrote a play, *Troilus and Cressida*, on
this subject.

Scene 1 *Belmont. The garden in front of Portia's house*

Enter Lorenzo *and* Jessica

Lorenzo
The moon shines bright: in such a night as this,
When the sweet wind did gently kiss the trees,
And they did make no noise, in such a night
Troilus methinks mounted the Trojan walls,
5 And sigh'd his soul toward the Grecian tents,
Where Cressid lay that night.
    Jessica   In such a night
Did Thisbe fearfully o'ertrip the dew,
And saw the lion's shadow ere himself,

7   *Thisbe*: when she saw the lion, Thisbe ran away, dropping her scarf which the lion mauled. Seeing the bloody scarf, her lover Pyramus thought Thisbe had been killed, and stabbed himself. This episode is made comic in Shakespeare's *A Midsummer Night's Dream*.

o'ertrip: walk lightly over.

8   *ere himself*: before she saw the lion.

10   *Dido*: the Queen of Carthage, who was deserted by her lover Aeneas when he sailed to Italy. Shakespeare's great contemporary, Christopher Marlowe, wrote a tragedy on this subject.

11   *waft*: waved to.

13   *Medea*: the enchantress who loved Jason and helped him to win the golden fleece (see note on *1, 1, 170*); she restored Aeson (Jason's father) to youth with her magic herbs.

15   *steal*: both 'run away' and 'rob'.

16   *unthrift love*: both 'careless devotion' and 'penniless lover'.

19   *Stealing*: gaining possession.

21   *shrew*: scolding woman.

23   *out-night you*: beat you at this game of 'in such a night'; the word is invented.

did nobody come: if there were not somebody coming.

24   *footing*: footsteps.

31   *holy crosses*: small shrines set by the roadside for travellers to pray; there are few in England now, but many remain in Italy.

And ran dismay'd away.

Lorenzo   In such a night

10 Stood Dido with a willow in her hand
Upon the wild sea-banks, and waft her love
To come again to Carthage.

Jessica   In such a night
Medea gather'd the enchanted herbs
That did renew old Æson.

Lorenzo   In such a night

15 Did Jessica steal from the wealthy Jew,
And with an unthrift love did run from Venice,
As far as Belmont.

Jessica   In such a night
Did young Lorenzo swear he lov'd her well,
Stealing her soul with many vows of faith,

20 And ne'er a true one.

Lorenzo   In such a night
Did pretty Jessica, like a little shrew,
Slander her love, and he forgave it her.

Jessica
I would out-night you, did nobody come;
But, hark! I hear the footing of a man.

Enter Stephano

Lorenzo

25 Who comes so fast in silence of the night?

Stephano
A friend.

Lorenzo
A friend! what friend? your name, I pray you, friend.

Stephano
Stephano is my name; and I bring word
My mistress will before the break of day

30 Be here at Belmont: she doth stray about
By holy crosses, where she kneels and prays
For happy wedlock hours.

Lorenzo   Who comes with her?

Stephano
None but a holy hermit and her maid.
I pray you, is my master yet return'd?

Lorenzo

35 He is not, nor we have not heard from him.
But go we in, I pray thee, Jessica,
And ceremoniously let us prepare
Some welcome for the mistress of the house.

Enter Launcelot

Launcelot

Sola, sola! wo ha, ho! sola, sola!

Lorenzo

40 Who calls?

Launcelot

Sola! did you see Master Lorenzo? Master
Lorenzo! sola, sola!

Lorenzo

Leave hollowing, man; here.

Launcelot

Sola! where? where?

Lorenzo

45 Here.

Launcelot

Tell him there's a post come from my master, with
his horn full of good news: my master will be here
ere morning.   [*Exit*

Lorenzo

Sweet soul, let's in, and there expect their coming.

50 And yet no matter; why should we go in?
My friend Stephano, signify, I pray you,
Within the house, your mistress is at hand;
And bring your music forth into the air.

[*Exit* Stephano

How sweet the moonlight sleeps upon this bank!

55 Here will we sit, and let the sounds of music
Creep in our ears: soft stillness and the night
Become the touches of sweet harmony.
Sit, Jessica—look how the floor of heaven
Is thick inlaid with patens of bright gold:

60 There's not the smallest orb which thou behold'st
But in his motion like an angel sings,
Still quiring to the young-eyed cherubins;
Such harmony is in immortal souls,
But whilst this muddy vesture of decay

65 Doth grossly close it in, we cannot hear it.

37-8   *ceremoniously . . . welcome*: let us
prepare some ceremony of welcome.

39   Launcelot is pretending to be
a messenger-boy blowing his horn.

43   *Leave hollowing*: stop shouting.

46   *post*: messenger.

51   *signify*: announce.

57   *Become*: suit.
59   *patens*: small pieces of shiny
metal—the stars.
60   *orb*: planet.
61   *motion*: movement. The Elizabethans believed that as the planets
moved they created heavenly harmony
but (as Lorenzo explains) human
beings could not hear it.
62   *quiring*: serenading.
young-eyed cherubins: angels
whose eyes are always young.
64   *vesture of decay*: clothing of
mortality—the human body.
65   *grossly*: roughly.

66   *Diana*: the classical goddess of the moon, who fell in love with the beautiful Endymion and came down from heaven every night to sleep with him (see also line 109).

70   *attentive*: receptive.

72   *race*: breed.
      unhandled: unbroken, untrained.

74   Which it is in the nature of their wild blood to do.

75   *perchance*: perhaps.

77   *make a mutual stand*: all stand still at once.

78   *modest*: gentle.

79–80 *the poet . . . floods*: the Roman poet Ovid told how Orpheus, a Greek musician, charmed even lifeless objects with his music.

81   *naught*: nothing.
      stockish: stubborn.

84   *concord*: harmony.

85   *stratagems*: plots.
      spoils: destruction.

86   *motions*: movements.

87   *Erebus*: a dark place in the Greek underworld.

88   *Mark*: pay attention to.

91   *naughty*: wicked.

94   *substitute*: deputy.

95   *by*: present.

95–6 *his state Empties itself*: his glory vanishes.

97   *main of waters*: sea.

98   *music . . . of the house*: a small company of musicians, belonging to Portia's household of servants.

Enter Musicians

Come, ho! and wake Diana with a hymn:
With sweetest touches pierce your mistress' ear,
And draw her home with music.   [*Music*
      Jessica
I am never merry when I hear sweet music.
      Lorenzo
70 The reason is, your spirits are attentive:
For do but note a wild and wanton herd,
Or race of youthful and unhandled colts,
Fetching mad bounds, bellowing and neighing loud,
Which is the hot condition of their blood;
75 If they but hear perchance a trumpet sound,
Or any air of music touch their ears,
You shall perceive them make a mutual stand,
Their savage eyes turn'd to a modest gaze
By the sweet power of music: therefore the poet
80 Did feign that Orpheus drew trees, stones, and floods;
Since naught so stockish, hard, and full of rage,
But music for the time doth change his nature.
The man that hath no music in himself,
Nor is not mov'd with concord of sweet sounds,
85 Is fit for treasons, stratagems, and spoils;
The motions of his spirit are dull as night,
And his affections dark as Erebus:
Let no such man be trusted. Mark the music.

Enter Portia *and* Nerissa
      Portia
That light we see is burning in my hall.
90 How far that little candle throws his beams!
So shines a good deed in a naughty world.
      Nerissa
When the moon shone, we did not see the candle.
      Portia
So doth the greater glory dim the less:
A substitute shines brightly as a king
95 Until a king be by, and then his state
Empties itself, as doth an inland brook
Into the main of waters. Music! hark!
      Nerissa
It is your music, madam, of the house.

99   Nothing is good in itself alone,
      without taking circumstances into
      consideration.

103   *attended*: listened to.
104   *nightingale*: a bird that sings only
      at night, when all other birds are silent.

107-8   *by season . . . perfection*: what
      a lot of things are given their proper
      value and excellence by the fact that
      they come at the right time.
109   *Endymion*: see note on 5, 1, 66.

115   And we hope that they have had
      some benefit from our prayers.

119-20   *take No note*: make no mention.

123   *tell-tales*: tellers of secrets.

127-8   It would be daytime here when
      it is in Australia ('the Antipodes' = the
      other side of the world) if you [Portia]
      would walk here when the sun is away.

Portia
Nothing is good, I see, without respect:
100 Methinks it sounds much sweeter than by day.
Nerissa
Silence bestows that virtue on it, madam.
Portia
The crow doth sing as sweetly as the lark
When neither is attended, and I think
The nightingale, if she should sing by day
105 When every goose is cackling, would be thought
No better a musician than the wren.
How many things by season season'd are
To their right praise and true perfection!
Peace, ho! the moon sleeps with Endymion,
110 And would not be awak'd!
                              [*Music ceases*
Lorenzo   That is the voice,
Or I am much deceiv'd, of Portia.
Portia
He knows me, as the blind man knows the cuckoo,
By the bad voice.
Lorenzo   Dear lady, welcome home.
Portia
We have been praying for our husbands' welfare,
115 Which speed, we hope, the better for our words.
Are they return'd?
Lorenzo   Madam, they are not yet;
But there is come a messenger before,
To signify their coming.
Portia   Go in, Nerissa:
Give order to my servants that they take
120 No note at all of our being absent hence;
Nor you, Lorenzo; Jessica, nor you.
                              [*A trumpet sounds*
Lorenzo
Your husband is at hand, I hear his trumpet;
We are no tell-tales, madam, fear you not.
Portia
This night methinks is but the daylight sick;
125 It looks a little paler: 'tis a day,
Such as the day is when the sun is hid.

      Enter Bassanio, Antonio, Gratiano, *and
      their* Servants
Bassanio
We should hold day with the Antipodes,
If you would walk in absence of the sun.

129 *be light*: be faithless.

130 *heavy*: sorrowful.

131 *for me*: because of what I have done.

132 *sort all*: decide everything.

135 *bound*: indebted.

137 *bound*: in chains as a prisoner.

138 *acquitted of*: repaid for (with the love of Bassanio and the gratitude of Portia).

141 *scant*: cut short.
breathing courtesy: verbal politeness.

144 *Would . . . gelt*: I wish he had been castrated.
for my part: as far as I am concerned.

145 Since it seems to mean so much to you.

148 *posy*: words engraved on a ring.

149 *cutler's poetry*: doggerel verse, engraved by a knife-maker ('cutler') on his knives.

151 *What*: why?

155 *for me*: for my sake.

156 *respective*: careful of your honour.

158 *wear hair on's face*: grow a beard.

159 *and if*: if ever.

Portia
Let me give light, but let me not be light;
130 For a light wife doth make a heavy husband,
And never be Bassanio so for me:
But God sort all! You are welcome home, my lord.
Bassanio
I thank you, madam. Give welcome to my friend:
This is the man, this is Antonio,
135 To whom I am so infinitely bound.
Portia
You should in all sense be much bound to him,
For, as I hear, he was much bound for you.
Antonio
No more than I am well acquitted of.
Portia
Sir, you are very welcome to our house:
140 It must appear in other ways than words,
Therefore I scant this breathing courtesy.
Gratiano
[*To* Nerissa] By yonder moon I swear you do me
    wrong;
In faith, I gave it to the judge's clerk;
Would he were gelt that had it, for my part,
145 Since you do take it, love, so much at heart.
Portia
A quarrel, ho, already! what's the matter?
Gratiano
About a hoop of gold, a paltry ring
That she did give me, whose posy was
For all the world like cutler's poetry
150 Upon a knife, 'Love me, and leave me not'.
Nerissa
What talk you of the posy, or the value?
You swore to me, when I did give it you,
That you would wear it till your hour of death,
And that it should lie with you in your grave:
155 Though not for me, yet for your vehement oaths,
You should have been respective and have kept it.
Gave it a judge's clerk! no, God's my judge,
The clerk will ne'er wear hair on's face that had it.
Gratiano
He will, and if he live to be a man.

Nerissa
160 Ay, if a woman live to be a man.

Gratiano
Now, by this hand, I gave it to a youth,
A kind of boy, a little scrubbed boy,
No higher than thyself, the judge's clerk.
A prating boy that begg'd it as a fee:
165 I could not for my heart deny it him.

Portia
You were to blame—I must be plain with you—
To part so slightly with your wife's first gift;
A thing stuck on with oaths upon your finger,
And so riveted with faith unto your flesh.
170 I gave my love a ring and made him swear
Never to part with it: and here he stands;
I dare be sworn for him he would not leave it,
Nor pluck it from his finger, for the wealth
That the world masters. Now, in faith, Gratiano,
175 You give your wife too unkind a cause of grief:
And 'twere to me, I should be mad at it.

Bassanio
[*Aside*] Why, I were best to cut my left hand off,
And swear I lost the ring defending it.

Gratiano
My Lord Bassanio gave his ring away
180 Unto the judge that begg'd it, and indeed
Deserv'd it too; and then the boy, his clerk,
That took some pains in writing, he begg'd mine;
And neither man nor master would take aught
But the two rings.

Portia   What ring gave you, my lord?
185 Not that, I hope, which you receiv'd of me.

Bassanio
If I could add a lie unto a fault,
I would deny it; but you see my finger
Hath not the ring upon it—it is gone.

Portia
Even so void is your false heart of truth.
190 By heaven, I will ne'er come in your bed
Until I see the ring.

Nerissa   Nor I in yours,
Till I again see mine.

162   *scrubbed*: stunted.

164   *prating*: chattering.

172   *leave*: part with.

174   *masters*: is master of.

176   *And 'twere to me*: if it had been done to me.

182   *pains*: care.

189   *void*: empty.

Bassanio   Sweet Portia,
If you did know to whom I gave the ring,
If you did know for whom I gave the ring,
195 And would conceive for what I gave the ring,
And how unwillingly I left the ring,
When naught would be accepted but the ring,
You would abate the strength of your displeasure.
Portia
If you had known the virtue of the ring,
200 Or half her worthiness that gave the ring,
Or your own honour to contain the ring,
You would not then have parted with the ring.
What man is there so much unreasonable,
If you had pleas'd to have defended it
205 With any terms of zeal, wanted the modesty
To urge the thing held as a ceremony?
Nerissa teaches me what to believe:
I'll die for 't, but some woman had the ring.
Bassanio
No, by my honour, madam, by my soul,
210 No woman had it, but a civil doctor,
Which did refuse three thousand ducats of me,
And begg'd the ring, the which I did deny him,
And suffer'd him to go displeas'd away;
Even he that had held up the very life
215 Of my dear friend. What should I say, sweet lady?
I was enforc'd to send it after him.
I was beset with shame and courtesy;
My honour would not let ingratitude
So much besmear it. Pardon me, good lady,
220 For by these blessed candles of the night,
Had you been there, I think you would have begg'd
The ring of me to give the worthy doctor.
Portia
Let not that doctor e'er come near my house.
Since he hath got the jewel that I lov'd,
225 And that which you did swear to keep for me;
I will become as liberal as you—
I'll not deny him anything I have,
No, not my body, nor my husband's bed.
Know him I shall, I am well sure of it.
230 Lie not a night from home; watch me like Argus:

199   *virtue*: magic power.

201   Or how it was a matter of honour that you should keep the ring.

205   *terms of zeal*: determination.
205-6   *wanted . . . ceremony*: would have been so lacking in good manners as to insist on having something that you thought sacred.
208   *I'll die for 't*: I am ready to die for my belief.
210   *civil doctor*: doctor of civil law.

213   *suffer'd*: allowed.
214   *held up*: saved.

217   *beset*: overcome.

219   *besmear*: stain.
220   *candles of the night*: i.e. the stars.

222   *of*: from.

230   *Argus*: in classical mythology, a monster with a hundred eyes.

If you do not, if I be left alone,
Now by mine honour, which is yet mine own,
I'll have that doctor for my bedfellow.

Nerissa
And I his clerk; therefore be well advis'd
235 How you do leave me to mine own protection.

Gratiano
Well, do you so: let not me take him, then,
For if I do, I'll mar the young clerk's pen.

Antonio
I am th' unhappy subject of these quarrels.

Portia
Sir, grieve not you; you are welcome notwithstanding.

Bassanio
240 Portia, forgive me this enforced wrong;
And in the hearing of these many friends,
I swear to thee, even by thine own fair eyes,
Wherein I see myself—

Portia   Mark you but that!
In both my eyes he doubly sees himself;
245 In each eye, one: swear by your double self,
And there's an oath of credit.

Bassanio   Nay, but hear me:
Pardon this fault, and by my soul I swear
I never more will break an oath with thee.

Antonio
I once did lend my body for his wealth,
250 Which, but for him that had your husband's ring,
Had quite miscarried: I dare be bound again,
My soul upon the forfeit, that your lord
Will never more break faith advisedly.

Portia
Then you shall be his surety. Give him this,
255 And bid him keep it better than the other.

Antonio
Here, Lord Bassanio; swear to keep this ring.

Bassanio
By heaven! it is the same I gave the doctor!

Portia
I had it of him: pardon me, Bassanio,
For, by this ring, the doctor lay with me.

234   *be well advis'd*: take good care.
235   *to mine own protection*: to look after my own honour.
236   *take*: catch.
237   *I'll mar . . . pen*: I'll ruin his equipment.

240   *this enforced wrong*: this injury that I was compelled to do.

246   *of credit*: that can be believed.

249   *wealth*: well-being, happiness.

251   *miscarried*: been lost.
252   *My . . . forfeit*: at the risk of forfeiting my soul.
253   *advisedly*: deliberately.
254   *surety*: security.

Nerissa

260 And pardon me, my gentle Gratiano;
For that same scrubbed boy, the doctor's clerk,
In lieu of this, last night did lie with me.

Gratiano

Why, this is like the mending of highways
In summer, where the ways are fair enough!

265 What, are we cuckolds ere we have deserv'd it?

Portia

Speak not so grossly. You are all amaz'd:
Here is a letter, read it at your leisure,
It comes from Padua, from Bellario:
There you shall find that Portia was the doctor,

270 Nerissa there her clerk. Lorenzo here
Shall witness I set forth as soon as you,
And even but now return'd; I have not yet
Enter'd my house. Antonio, you are welcome;
And I have better news in store for you

275 Than you expect: unseal this letter soon;
There you shall find three of your argosies
Are richly come to harbour suddenly.
You shall not know by what strange accident
I chanced on this letter.

Antonio   I am dumb.

Bassanio

280 Were you the doctor, and I knew you not?

Gratiano

Were you the clerk that is to make me cuckold?

Nerissa

Ay, but the clerk that never means to do it,
Unless he live until he be a man.

Bassanio

Sweet doctor, you shall be my bedfellow:

285 When I am absent, then lie with my wife.

Antonio

Sweet lady, you have given me life and living;
For here I read for certain that my ships
Are safely come to road.

Portia   How now, Lorenzo!
My clerk hath some good comforts too for you.

---

262   *In lieu of*: in return for.
263-4   Newly-married wives should not need to take lovers—any more than roads should need mending in summer.
265   *cuckolds*: men whose wives are unfaithful to them.
      deserv'd it: i.e. by showing themselves to be unsatisfactory lovers.
266   *grossly*: coarsely.

275   *soon*: at once.
276   *argosies*: merchant ships.

288   *road*: anchorage.

Nerissa

290 Ay, and I'll give them him without a fee.
There do I give to you and Jessica,
From the rich Jew, a special deed of gift,
After his death, of all he dies possess'd of.

Lorenzo

Fair ladies, you drop manna in the way
295 Of starved people.

Portia   It is almost morning,
And yet I am sure you are not satisfied
Of these events at full. Let us go in;
And charge us there upon inter'gatories,
And we will answer all things faithfully.

Gratiano

300 Let it be so: the first inter'gatory
That my Nerissa shall be sworn on is,
Whether till the next night she had rather stay,
Or go to bed now, being two hours to day:
But were the day come, I should wish it dark,
305 That I were couching with the doctor's clerk.
Well, while I live, I'll fear no other thing
So sore as keeping safe Nerissa's ring.   [*Exeunt*

294   *manna*: food which the Israelites found when they were starving in the wilderness and which they believed to have been sent from heaven (Exodus 16: 14).
298   *at full*: in detail.
299   Ask us for our information (interrogate us) as though we were witnesses in court.

305   *couching*: going to bed.
306   *while I live*: as long as I live.
306-7   *I'll . . . ring*: I'll take care of nothing so much as guarding Nerissa's ring [and also her honour].

Sources

The lady, the pound of flesh, and the ring

The most likely source for the main plot in *The Merchant of Venice* seems to have been one of the stories in *Il Pecorone*, a collection of tales by Ser Giovanni Fiorentino, which was published at Milan in 1558. No English version has ever been found — so we must assume that Shakespeare read the original in Italian.

Ansaldo, a wealthy merchant of Venice, financed his godson Giannetto in his attempts to win the Lady of Belmont. This Lady was a rich widow who had agreed to marry the first man who succeeded in making love to her — but she had imposed the condition that all unsuccessful lovers must forfeit everything they possessed. Giannetto twice attempted this task; and both times he failed — because he was given drugged wine to make him fall asleep before the lady came to bed. Because he was ashamed of his failures, he told Ansaldo that he had twice been shipwrecked. Determined to make a third attempt, he begged Ansaldo for more money. This time Ansaldo was forced to borrow ten thousand ducats from a Jew to enable him to equip yet another ship for Giannetto. The Jew made the condition that if the loan were not repaid upon St John's Day, the merchant would forfeit a pound of his own flesh.

Giannetto (warned by a maid not to drink the drugged wine) succeeded in making love to the lady; he married her, and was proclaimed sovereign of all that she possessed. He forgot about Ansaldo's bargain with the Jew until St John's Day arrived, and then he told his wife the whole story. The Lady sent Giannetto to Venice with enough money to repay the Jew; and she herself followed him, disguised as a lawyer.

The Jew refused to accept Giannetto's money, because he wanted to say that he had killed the greatest of all the Christian merchants. The 'lawyer' claimed that she could settle all disputes, and she heard the Jew's case against Ansaldo, with Giannetto's offer to repay the debt. She advised the Jew to take the ten thousand ducats, but he persisted in refusing. She then told him to take the pound of flesh — but, at the last moment, she warned him that if he took more than an exact pound, or shed one drop of blood, he would be executed. The Jew then asked for the money instead of the flesh. When this was refused, he tore up the bond.

Giannetto offered the ducats as a fee to the 'lawyer', but she demanded to be given his ring. He then returned to Belmont, taking Ansaldo with him. The Lady accused Giannetto of giving the ring to one of his former mistresses. He wept, but finally the Lady explained everything — and Ansaldo married the maid who had warned Giannetto about the drugged wine.

The caskets

The casket story may have been suggested by the account in History 32 of *Gesta Romanorum*, translated by R. Robinson in 1595, where the heroine was told to make a choice between three 'vessels' in order to win a husband.

'The first [vessel] was made of pure gold, well-beset with precious stones without, and within full of dead mens' bones; and thereupon was engraved this poesy: *Whoso chooseth me shall find that he deserveth*. The second vessel was made of fine silver, filled with earth and worms; and the superscription was thus: *Whoso chooseth me shall find that his nature desireth*. The third vessel was made of lead, full within of precious stones; and thereupon was ensculped this poesy: *Whoso chooseth me, shall find that God hath disposed for him.*'

The Jew and his daughter

A contemporary play, *The Jew of Malta* (c. 1589) by Christopher Marlowe, gave Shakespeare some inspiration for the character of Shylock. Marlowe's Jew, Barabas, is determined to be revenged on the Christians who persecute him; and he too has a daughter who loves a Christian. Shylock's lament — 'My daughter! O my ducats! O my daughter!' (2, 8, 15) — seems to be modelled on Barabas's cry: 'Oh my girl! My gold, my fortune . . . Oh girl! Oh gold! Oh beauty! Oh my bliss!' (2, 2, 47–54).

Classwork and Examinations

The works of Shakespeare are studied all over the world, and this classroom edition is being used in many different countries. Teaching methods vary from school to school and there are many different ways of examining a student's work. Some teachers and examiners expect detailed knowledge of Shakespeare's text; others ask for imaginative involvement with his characters and their situations; and there are some teachers who want their students to share in the theatrical experience of directing and performing a play. Most people use a variety of methods. This section of the book offers a few suggestions for approaches to *The Merchant of Venice* which could be used in schools and colleges to help with students' understanding and *enjoyment* of the play.

    A Discussion
    B Character Study
    C Activities
    D Context Questions
    E Comprehension Questions
    F Essays
    G Projects

A Discussion

Talking about the play — about the issues it raises and the characters who are involved — is one of the most rewarding and pleasurable aspects of the study of Shakespeare. It makes sense to discuss each scene as it is read, sharing impressions — and perhaps correcting misapprehensions. It can be useful to compare aspects of this play with other fictions — plays, novels, films — or with modern life.

Suggestions

A1 Bassanio borrows money from Antonio, and Antonio borrows from Shylock. Antonio disapproves of Shylock because he charges interest on his loans; and Shylock grumbles because Antonio 'lends out money gratis' (*1*, 3, 40). What is *your* attitude to borrowing and lending?

A2   Portia's father, even though he is dead, has power over his daughter's choice of husband — 'the will of a living daughter is curbed by the will of a dead father' (*1*, 2, 24). Do you think that parents — alive or dead — should have any influence over their children's marriages?

A3   Jessica, a Jew, marries Lorenzo, a Christian; do you approve of such 'mixed' marriages?

A4   'All things that are, Are with more spirit chased than enjoy'd' (*2*, 6, 12–3). How true is this?

A5   Shylock demands justice, but Portia advocates mercy (*Act 4, Scene 1*). Discuss justice and mercy in the world of the twentieth century.

B   Character Study

Shakespeare is famous for his creation of characters who seem like real people. We can judge their actions and we can try to understand their thoughts and feelings — just as we criticize and try to understand the people we know. As the play progresses, we learn to like or dislike, love or hate, them — just as though they lived in *our* world.

Characters can be studied *from the outside*, by observing what they do, and listening sensitively to what they say. This is the scholar's method: the scholar — or any reader — has access to the whole play, and can see the function of every character within the whole scheme of that play.

Another approach works *from the inside*, taking a single character and looking at the action and the other characters from his/her point of view. This is an actor's technique when creating, for performance, a personality who can have only a partial view of what is going on. This method asks for a student's inventive imagination. The two methods — both useful in different ways — are really complementary to each other.

Suggestions

a) from 'outside' the character

B1   Is it possible to characterize Salerio and Solanio? What is their function in the play?

B2   'I have much ado to know myself' (Antonio, *1*, 1, 7). How well do we get to *know* Antonio?

B3 Do you find Bassanio an attractive — and *coherent* — character?

B4 Describe the character of Gratiano, and say what you think he contributes to the play.

B5 Does the play need Launcelot Gobbo and his father?

B6 How sympathetic are you to Shylock?

b) from 'inside' a character

B7 In the character of Antonio, speak your thoughts in soliloquy at the end of *Act 1*, Scene 1, or confide them to your diary.

B8 As Bassanio, give your reasons — in a modern idiom — for your choice of caskets.

B9 Imagine that you are a servant who is present when one of the caskets is opened. Describe the scene, and the characters involved, in a letter to your friend.

B10 Write a letter from Jessica to her girl-friend, recounting her adventures with Lorenzo.

B11 In the character of Nerissa, describe how you went to the court in Venice and what it was that you saw and heard there.

C Activities

These can involve two or more students, preferably working *away from* the desk or study-table and using gesture and position ('body-language') as well as speech. They can help students to develop a sense of drama and the dramatic aspects of Shakespeare's play — which was written to be *performed*, not studied in a classroom.

Suggestions

C1 Act the play, or at least some parts of it. Try expressing Shakespeare's thoughts in your own words.

C2 Devise a scene for Salerio and Solanio in which they can discuss Antonio's strange moods.

C3 The engagement of Gratiano and Nerissa seems to take everyone by surprise at the end of *Act 3*, Scene 2. Plan a scene (or scenes) to show how their love develops.

C4 Arraign Antonio before the Race Relations Board.

C5   The trial of Antonio is a very important event in Venice. Give it full 'media coverage' — newspaper, radio, and television (with signing for the deaf, if possible).

D   Context Questions

In written examinations, these questions present you with short passages from the play, and ask you to explain them. They are intended to test your knowledge of the play and your understanding of its words. Usually you have to make a choice of passages: there may be five on the paper, and you are asked to choose three. Be very sure that you know exactly how many passages you must choose. Study the ones offered to you, and select those you feel most certain of. Make your answers accurate and concise — don't waste time writing more than the examiner is asking for.

D1   The patch is kind enough, but a huge feeder;
Snail-slow in profit, and he sleeps by day
More than the wild-cat: drones hive not with me;
Therefore I part with him, and part with him
To one that I would have him help to waste
His borrow'd purse.

    (i) Who is speaking, and to whom does he speak?
   (ii) Who is being discussed, and what has this person decided to do?
  (iii) How does the person addressed feel towards the speaker?

D2   You know me well, and herein spend but time
To wind about my love with circumstance;
And out of doubt you do me now more wrong
In making question of my uttermost
Than if you had made waste of all I have.
Then do but say to me what I should do.

    (i) Who is speaking, and to whom does he speak?
   (ii) What is the speaker accusing the other person of?
  (iii) What does the person addressed want the speaker to do, and why?

D3   O, be thou damn'd, inexorable dog!
And for thy life let justice be accus'd.

Thou almost mak'st me waver in my faith
To hold opinion with Pythagoras,
That souls of animals infuse themselves
Into the trunks of men: thy currish spirit
Govern'd a wolf.

(i) Who is speaking, and on what occasion?
(ii) What has the person addressed been doing to cause this outburst?
(iii) What effect does this speech have on the person addressed?

D4 Lock up my doors, and when you hear the drum
And the vile squealing of the wry-neck'd fife,
Clamber not you up to the casements then,
Nor thrust your head into the public street
To gaze on Christian fools with varnish'd faces,
But stop my house's ears — I mean my casements —
Let not the sound of shallow fopp'ry enter
My sober house.

(i) Who is speaking, and to whom does he speak?
(ii) Where is the speaker going?
(iii) How will the 'Christian fools with varnish'd faces' help the person addressed?

D5 You swore to me when I did give it you,
That you would wear it till your hour of death,
And that it should lie with you in your grave:
Though not for me, yet for your vehement oaths,
You should have been respective and have kept it.
Gave it a judge's clerk! no, God's my judge,
The clerk will ne'er wear hair on's face that had it.

(i) Two people are quarrelling: who are they?
(ii) What does 'it' refer to?
(iii) Will the 'clerk' ever 'wear hair' on his face? Why?

D6 I am as like to call thee so again,
To spit on thee again, to spurn thee too.
If thou wilt lend this money, lend it not
As to thy friends, for when did friendship take
A breed for barren metal of his friend?

But lend it rather to thine enemy;
Who if he break, thou may'st with better face
Exact the penalty.

  (i) Who is speaking, and to whom does he speak?
 (ii) Why will the speaker spit on the man he addresses?
(iii) What is meant by 'if he break'? Will the speaker ever
      'break'?

E Comprehension Questions

These also present passages from the play and ask questions about
them, and again you often have a choice of passages. But the
extracts are much longer than those presented as context questions.
A detailed knowledge of the language of the play is asked for here,
and you must be able to express unusual or archaic phrases in your
own words; you may also be asked to comment critically on the
effectiveness of Shakespeare's language.

E1 *Portia*
       You see me, Lord Bassanio, where I stand,
       Such as I am: though for myself alone
       I would not be ambitious in my wish,
       To wish myself much better; yet, for you,
       I would be trebled twenty times myself;   5
       A thousand times more fair, ten thousand times
            more rich;
       That only to stand high in your account,
       I might in virtues, beauties, livings, friends,
       Exceed account: but the full sum of me
       Is sum of something, which, to term in gross,   10
       Is an unlesson'd girl, unschool'd, unpractis'd,
       Happy in this, she is not yet so old
       But she may learn; happier than this,
       She is not bred so dull but she can learn;
       Happiest of all, is that her gentle spirit   15
       Commits itself to yours to be directed
       As from her lord, her governor, her king.
       Myself and what is mine, to you and yours
       Is now converted: but now I was the lord
       Of this fair mansion, master of my servants,   20
       Queen o'er myself; and even now, but now,

This house, these servants, and this same myself
Are yours, my lord's. I give them with this ring;
Which when you part from, lose, or give away,
Let it presage the ruin of your love,   25
And be my vantage to exclaim on you.

   (i) Say exactly where in the play this passage occurs.
  (ii) Give the meaning of 'livings' (line 8), 'happy' (line 12),
      'but now' (line 19), and 'presage' (line 25).
 (iii) Express in your own words the meaning of line 7 ('only
      . . . account'), lines 18–19 ('Myself . . . converted'), and
      line 26 ('be my vantage . . . you').
  (iv) What happens to the ring that Portia gives to Bassanio in
      line 23?
   (v) What impression of the relationship between Portia and
      Bassanio do you get from this passage?

E2 *Arragon*
I will not choose what many men desire,
Because I will not jump with common spirits
And rank me with the barbarous multitudes.
Why, then to thee, thou silver treasure house;
Tell me once more what title thou dost bear: 5
'*Who chooseth me shall get as much as he deserves*'.
And well said too; for who shall go about
To cozen fortune, and be honourable
Without the stamp of merit? Let none presume
To wear an undeserved dignity.   10
O that estates, degrees, and offices
Were not deriv'd corruptly, and that clear honour
Were purchas'd by the merit of the wearer.
How many then should cover that stand bare!
How many be commanded that command!   15
How much low peasantry would then be glean'd
From the true seed of honour! and how much honour
Pick'd from the chaff and ruin of the times
To be new varnish'd! Well, but to my choice:
'*Who chooseth me shall get as much as he deserves*'.   20
I will assume desert. Give me the key for this,
And instantly unlock my fortunes here.

   (i) What does the Prince of Arragon find in the casket?
  (ii) Give the meaning of 'title' (line 5), 'cozen' (line 8), and
      'assume desert' (line 21).

(iii) Express in your own words the meaning of lines 2–3 ('Because . . . multitudes'), line 14 ('How . . . bare'), lines 16–17 ('How much . . . honour'), and lines 17–19 ('and how much honour . . . varnish'd').
(iv) What is the dramatic necessity for the scene in which this speech occurs?
(v) Describe the Prince of Arragon's character as it is revealed in this speech and elsewhere in the scene.

E3 *Lorenzo*
How sweet the moonlight sleeps upon this bank!
Here will we sit, and let the sounds of music
Creep in our ears: soft stillness and the night
Become the touches of sweet harmony.
Sit, Jessica — look how the floor of heaven   5
Is thick inlaid with patens of bright gold;
There's not the smallest orb which thou behold'st
But in his motion like an angel sings,
Still quiring to the young-eyed cherubins;
Such harmony is in immortal souls,   10
But whilst this muddy vesture of decay
Doth grossly close it in, we cannot hear it.
              Enter Musicians
Come, ho! and wake Diana with a hymn:
With sweetest touches pierce your mistress' ear,
And draw her home with music.   15

(i) Say exactly where in the play this speech occurs.
(ii) Give the meaning of 'Become' (line 4), 'patens' (line 6), 'quiring' (line 9), and 'cherubins' (line 9).
(iii) Explain the meaning of lines 7–8 ('There's not . . . sings'), line 11–12 ('But whilst . . . hear it'), and line 13 ('wake Diana with a hymn').
(iv) What are Jessica and Lorenzo doing at Belmont?
(v) What is the dramatic function of the first part of the scene in which this speech occurs?

F   Essays

These will usually give you a specific topic to discuss, or perhaps a question that must be answered, in writing, *with a reasoned argument*. They *never* want you to tell the story of the play — so don't!

Your examiner — or teacher — has read the play and does not need to be reminded of it. Relevant quotations will always help you to make your points more strongly.

F1 Do you agree that 'Portia is the most important character in the play'?

F2 Show how Shakespeare makes a contrast between Venice and Belmont.

F3 With detailed reference to the text of the play, describe the conflict between Antonio and Shylock.

F4 Describe *three* of Portia's suitors (other than Bassanio) and her attitudes towards them.

F5 In what ways is the sub-plot of Jessica and Lorenzo necessary to *The Merchant of Venice*?

F6 In Shakespeare's day, an alternative title for *The Merchant of Venice* was *The Jew of Venice*; which title do you think is the more appropriate?

G Projects

In some schools, students are asked to do more 'free-ranging' work, which takes them outside the text — but which should always be relevant to the play. Such Projects may demand skills other than reading and writing: design and artwork, for instance, may be involved. Sometimes a 'portfolio' of work is assembled over a considerable period of time; and this can be presented to the examiner as part of the student's work for assessment.

The availability of resources will, obviously, do much to determine the nature of the Projects; but this is something that only the local teachers will understand. However, there is always help to be found in libraries, museums, and art galleries.

G1 Venice.

G2 Famous Actors and Actresses in *The Merchant of Venice*.

G3 Shakespeare's Theatre.

G4 Women in Shakespeare's England.

G5 Moneylenders.

Background

England c. 1599

When Shakespeare was writing *The Merchant of Venice*, most people believed that the sun went round the earth. They were taught that this was a divinely ordered scheme of things, and that — in England — God had instituted a Church and ordained a Monarchy for the right government of the land and the populace.

'The past is a foreign country; they do things differently there.'

L.P. Hartley

Government

For most of Shakespeare's life, the reigning monarch was Queen Elizabeth I. With her counsellors and ministers she governed the country (population about five million) from London, although fewer than half a million people inhabited the capital city. In the rest of the country, law and order were maintained by the land-owners and enforced by their deputies. The average man had no vote — and his wife had no rights at all.

Religion

At this time, England was a Christian country. All children were baptized, soon after they were born, into the Church of England; they were taught the essentials of the Christian faith, and instructed in their duty to God and to humankind. Marriages were performed, and funerals conducted, only by the licensed clergy and in accordance with the Church's rites and ceremonies. Attendance at divine service was compulsory; absences (without good — medical — reason) could be punished by fines. By such means, the authorities were able to keep some check on the populace — recording births, marriages, and deaths; being alert to any religious nonconformity, which could be politically dangerous; and ensuring a minimum of orthodox instruction through the official 'Homilies' which were regularly preached from the pulpits of all parish churches throughout the realm. Following Henry VIII's break away from the Church of Rome, all people in England were able to hear the church services *in their own language*. The Book of Common Prayer was used in every church, and an English translation of the Bible was read aloud in public. The Christian religion had never been so well taught before!

Education

School education reinforced the Church's teaching. From the age of four, boys might attend the 'petty school' (French *'petite école'*) to learn the rudiments of reading and writing along with a few prayers; some schools also included work with numbers. At the age of seven, the boy was ready for the grammar school (if his father was willing and able to pay the fees). A thorough grounding in Latin grammar was followed by translation work and the study of Roman authors, paying attention as much to style as to matter. The arts of fine writing were thus inculcated from early youth.

A very few students proceeded to university; these were either clever scholarship boys, or else the sons of noblemen. Girls stayed at home, and acquired domestic and social skills — cooking, sewing, perhaps even music. The lucky ones might learn to read and write.

Language

At the start of the sixteenth century the English had a very poor opinion of their own language: there was little serious writing in English, and hardly any literature. Latin was the language of international scholarship, and Englishmen admired the eloquence of the Romans. They made many translations, and in this way they extended the resources of their own language, increasing its vocabulary and stretching its grammatical structures. French, Italian, and Spanish works were also translated, and — for the first time — there were English versions of the Bible. By the end of the century, English was a language to be proud of: it was rich in synonyms, capable of infinite variety and subtlety, and ready for all kinds of word-play — especially the *puns*, for which Shakespeare's English is renowned.

Drama

The great art-form of the Elizabethan period was its drama. The Elizabethans inherited a tradition of play-acting from the Middle Ages, and they reinforced this by reading and translating the

Roman playwrights. At the beginning of the sixteenth century, plays were performed by groups of actors, all-male companies (boys acted the female roles) who travelled from town to town, setting up their stages in open places (such as inn-yards) or, with the permission of the owner, in the hall of some noble house. The touring companies continued, in the provinces, into the seventeenth century; but in London, in 1576, a new building was erected for the performance of plays. This was the Theatre, the first purpose-built playhouse in England. Other playhouses followed (including Shakespeare's own theatre, the Globe); and the English drama reached new heights of eloquence.

There were those who disapproved, of course. The theatres, which brought large crowds together, could encourage the spread of disease — and dangerous ideas. During the summer, when the plague was at its worst, the playhouses were closed. A constant censorship was imposed, more or less severe at different times. The Puritan faction tried to close down the theatres, but — partly because there was royal favour for the drama, and partly because the buildings were outside the city limits — they did not succeed until 1642.

Theatre

From contemporary comments and sketches — most particularly a drawing by a Dutch visitor, Johannes de Witt — it is possible to form some idea of the typical Elizabethan playhouse for which most of Shakespeare's plays were written. Hexagonal in shape, it had three roofed galleries encircling an open courtyard. The plain, high stage projected into the yard, where it was surrounded by the audience of standing 'groundlings'. At the back were two doors for the actors' entrances and exits; and above these doors was a balcony — useful for a musicians' gallery or for the acting of scenes *above*. Over the stage was a thatched roof, supported on two pillars, forming a canopy — which seems to have been painted with the sun, moon and stars for the 'heavens'.

Underneath was space (concealed by curtaining) which could be used by characters ascending and descending through a trap-door in the stage. Costumes and properties were kept backstage, in the 'tiring house'. The actors dressed lavishly, often wearing the secondhand clothes bestowed by rich patrons. Stage properties were important for defining a location, but the dramatist's own words were needed to explain the time of day, since all performances took place in the early afternoon.

Selected Further Reading

Source

Muir, Kenneth, *The Sources of Shakespeare's Plays*, (London, 1977).

Bullough, Geoffrey, *Narrative and Dramatic Sources of Shakespeare*, 8 volumes, (London, 1957–75).

Criticism

Bradbrook, Muriel C., *The Growth and Structure of Elizabethan Comedy*, (London, 1955).

Burckhardt, Sigurd, 'The Merchant of Venice: The Gentle Bond', *Journal of English Literary History*, 29 (1962), 239–62.

Charlton, H.B., *Shakespearian Comedy*, (London, 1938).

Geary, Keith, 'The Nature of Portia's Victory: Turning to Men in *The Merchant of Venice*', *Shakespeare Survey* 37 (1984), 58–73.

Hapgood, Robert, 'Portia and the Merchant of Venice', *Modern Language Quarterly*, 28 (1967), 19–32.

Hill, R.F., '*The Merchant of Venice* and the Pattern of Romantic Comedy', *Shakespeare Survey* 28 (1975), 75–87.

Lever, J.W., 'Shylock, Portia and the Values of Shakespearian Comedy', *Shakespeare Quarterly*, 3 (1952), 383–8.

Midgley, Graham, '*The Merchant of Venice*: A Reconsideration', *Essays in Criticism*, 10, (1960), 119–33.

Moody, A.D., *Shakespeare: 'The Merchant of Venice'*, *Arnold Studies in English Literature*, 21 (London, 1964).

Background Reading

Blake, N.F., *Shakespeare's Language: an Introduction*, (Methuen, 1983).

Muir, K., and Schoenbaum, S., *A New Companion to Shakespeare Studies*, (Cambridge, 1971).

Schoenbaum, S., *William Shakespeare: A Documentary Life*, (Oxford, 1975).

Thomson, Peter, *Shakespeare's Theatre*, (Routledge and Kegan Paul, 1983).

William Shakespeare, 1564-1616

Elizabeth I was Queen of England when Shakespeare was born in 1564. He was the son of a tradesman who made and sold gloves in the small town of Stratford-upon-Avon, and he was educated at the grammar school in that town. Shakespeare did not go to university when he left school, but worked, perhaps, in his father's business. When he was eighteen he married Anne Hathaway, who became the mother of his daughter, Susanna, in 1583, and of twins in 1585.

There is nothing exciting, or even unusual, in this story; and from 1585 until 1592 there are no documents that can tell us anything at all about Shakespeare. But we have learned that in 1592 he was known in London, and that he had become both an actor and a playwright.

We do not know when Shakespeare wrote his first play, and indeed we are not sure of the order in which he wrote his works. If you look on page 108 at the list of his writings and their approximate dates, you will see how he started by writing plays on subjects taken from the history of England. No doubt this was partly because he was always an intensely patriotic man—but he was also a very shrewd business-man. He could see that the theatre audiences enjoyed being shown their own history, and it was certain that he would make a profit from this kind of drama.

The plays in the next group are mainly comedies, with romantic love stories of young people who fall in love with one another, and at the end of the play marry and live happily ever after.

At the end of the sixteenth century the happiness disappears, and Shakespeare's plays become melancholy, bitter, and tragic. This change may have been caused by some sadness in the writer's life (one of his twins died in 1596). Shakespeare, however, was not the only writer whose works at this time were very serious. The whole of England was facing a crisis. Queen Elizabeth I was growing old. She was greatly loved, and the people were sad to think she must soon die; they were also afraid, for the Queen had never married, and so there was no child to succeed her.

When James I came to the throne in 1603, Shakespeare continued to write serious drama—the great tragedies and the plays based on Roman history (such as *Julius Caesar*) for which he is most famous. Finally, before he retired from the theatre, he wrote another set of comedies. These all have the same theme: they tell of happiness which is lost, and then found again.

Shakespeare returned from London to Stratford, his home town. He was rich and successful, and he owned one of the biggest houses in the town. He died in 1616.

Shakespeare also wrote two long poems, and a collection of sonnets. The sonnets describe two love-affairs, but we do not know who the lovers were. Although there are many public documents concerned with his career as a writer and a business-man, Shakespeare has hidden his personal life from us. A nineteenth-century poet, Matthew Arnold, addressed Shakespeare in a poem, and wrote 'We ask and ask—Thou smilest, and art still'.

There is not even a trustworthy portrait of the world's greatest dramatist.

Approximate order of composition of Shakespeare's works

Period	Comedies	History plays	Tragedies	Poems
I	Comedy of Errors Taming of the Shrew Two Gentlemen of Verona Love's Labour's Lost	Henry VI, part 1 Henry VI, part 2 Henry VI, part 3 Richard III King John	Titus Andronicus	Venus and Adonis Rape of Lucrece
1594				
II	Midsummer Night's Dream Merchant of Venice Merry Wives of Windsor Much Ado About Nothing As You Like It	Richard II Henry IV, part 1 Henry IV, part 2 Henry V	Romeo and Juliet	Sonnets
1599				
III	Twelfth Night Troilus and Cressida Measure for Measure All's Well That Ends Well		Julius Caesar Hamlet Othello Timon of Athens King Lear Macbeth Antony and Cleopatra Coriolanus	
1608				
IV	Pericles Cymbeline The Winter's Tale The Tempest	Henry VIII		
1613				